Microsoft® OFFICE 2010

INTRODUCTORY WORKBOOK

Gary B. Shelly

Dave Nuscher

COURSE TECHNOLOGY
CENGAGE Learning™

Australia • Brazil • Japan • Korea • Mexico • Singapore • Spain • United Kingdom • United States

COURSE TECHNOLOGY
CENGAGE Learning

Microsoft® Office 2010: Introductory Workbook
Gary B. Shelly, Dave Nuscher

Vice President, Publisher: Nicole Pinard
Executive Editor: Kathleen McMahon
Product Manger: Aimee Poirier
Editorial Assistant: Angela Giannopoulos
Director of Marketing: Cheryl Costantini
Marketing Manager: Tristen Kendall
Marketing Coordinator: Adrienne Fung
Print Buyer: Julio Esperas
Director of Production: Patty Stephan
Content Project Manager: Matthew Hutchinson
Proofreader: Suzanne Huizenga
Art Director: Marissa Falco
Cover Designer: Lisa Kuhn, Curio Press, LLC
Cover Photo: Tom Kates Photography
Compositor: PreMediaGlobal

Library of Congress Control Number: 2010938082

ISBN-13: 978-1-4390-7844-0

ISBN-10: 1-4390-7844-0

Course Technology
20 Channel Center Street
Boston, MA 02210
USA

Cengage Learning is a leading provider of customized learning solutions with office locations around the globe, including Singapore, the United Kingdom, Australia, Mexico, Brazil, and Japan. Locate your local office at:
international.cengage.com/region

Cengage Learning products are represented in Canada by Nelson Education, Ltd.

For your course and learning solutions, visit **www.cengage.com**

To learn more about Course Technology, visit
www.cengage.com/coursetechnology

Purchase any of our products at your local college bookstore or at our preferred online store at **www.cengagebrain.com**

Printed in the United States of America
2 3 4 5 6 7 15 14 13 12 11

CONTENTS

⊙ CHAPTER THREE

Microsoft Office Outlook 2010

⊙ CHAPTER ONE

⊙ CHAPTER TWO

PREFACE

This Workbook is intended as a supplement to *Microsoft Office 2010: Introductory* by Gary Shelly and Misty Vermaat. A variety of activities are provided in a format that is easy to follow and facilitates learning the material presented by helping students recall, review, and master introductory Microsoft Office 2010 concepts and techniques.

Each chapter in the Workbook includes:

- An **Overview** summarizing the chapter's content and containing a partial chapter outline designed to be completed by the students. The chapter outline helps students identify, organize, and recognize relationships between important concepts.
- A **Review** that assists students in assessing their mastery of the subject matter through Matching, True/False, Modified True/False, Definition, Complete the Table, Screen Identification, Dialog Box, Multiple Choice, Fill in the Blanks, Sequence, and Short Answer questions.
- **Activities** calculated to help students develop a deeper understanding of the information in each chapter through Expanding on the Apply Your Knowledge/Make It Right/Lab exercises.

In addition to the activities in each chapter, the Workbook also offers a To the Student section that provides tips on using the textbook effectively, attending class, preparing for and taking tests, and using the Workbook.

TO THE STUDENT

Would you like to be promised success in this course? Your textbook, *Microsoft Office 2010: Introductory*, can be a source of the knowledge you will need to excel. Unfortunately, no textbook alone can guarantee mastery of the subject matter. To a great extent, genuine understanding depends on how hard you are willing to work. There are other resources available, however, that can help you to get the most out of this course. That is the intent of this Workbook.

Following are tips on using the textbook, attending class, preparing for and taking tests, and using this Workbook. Most of the tips in the first three areas will not only help to improve your performance in this course, they also can be applied to many of your other classes. The tips in the last area are designed to explain how this Workbook can enhance your understanding of the material in *Microsoft Office 2010: Introductory*.

Using the Textbook

The textbook is one of your most important tools in building a solid foundation in the subject matter. To use your textbook most effectively, follow these guidelines:

Survey the whole textbook first. The table of contents supplies an overview of the topics covered in the textbook. The preface explains the textbook's goals, objectives, pedagogical approach, organization, and student activities. As you scan the textbook, see how chapters are arranged, the way key terms and concepts are indicated, where illustrations and tables are used, and the types of exercises that conclude each chapter. Check how the index can be used to clarify information.

Start by skimming the chapter. Study the chapter objectives, which identify what you are expected to learn. Read the chapter introduction, which gives you a general idea of the chapter's content. Next, skim the chapter. Look at the section headings to get a feeling for how sections are related to each other. Notice bold or italic text; usually, these words are important. Finally, read the brief summary at the end of the chapter. The summary restates, in broad terms, the major concepts and conclusions offered in the chapter.

Carefully read the entire chapter. Some instructors prefer that you only skim a chapter before class and then do a detailed reading after their lecture. Other instructors want you to read the chapter thoroughly before class. Whenever you sit down to read the entire chapter, it may help first to review the exercises at the end of the chapter to provide a more specific focus for your reading. Read the two-page briefs that introduce each chapter in *Microsoft Office 2010: Introductory*. As you read through the rest of the chapter, make sure you understand all of the key terms and concepts. Pay particular attention to illustrations (screens, diagrams, and tables) and their captions; often, they help clarify ideas in the text. Write in your textbook — highlight important points, note relationships, and jot questions. Study the BTWs and Q&As that are scattered throughout each chapter. Thoughtfully examine the summary material (What You Should Know). Use the Office 2010 Learn It Online Web page to review and expand on the topics covered (Learn It Online). If there is anything you do not remember or understand, go back and reread the relevant sections. Do the guided exercise that builds on the material presented in the chapter (Apply Your Knowledge). Finally, complete any assigned additional exercises (Extend Your Knowledge, Make It Right, In the Lab, Cases and Places).

Attending Class

Attending class is a key ingredient for success in a course. Simply showing up, however, is not enough. To get the most out of class, follow these guidelines:

Arrive early and prepared. Sit close enough to the front of the room so that you can hear well and see any visual materials, such as slides or transparencies, clearly. Make sure you have necessary supplies, such as a notebook, writing implement, and your textbook. Be ready to start when your instructor begins.

Take notes. For most people, note-taking is essential to recall later the material presented in class. Note-taking styles vary: some people just jot down keywords and concepts, while others write more detailed narratives. The important thing is that the style you adopt works for you. If, when you later consult your notes, you find they do little to help you remember the subject of the lecture, try to be more comprehensive. If you find that in taking notes you frequently fall behind your instructor, try to be briefer. Many people review their notes as soon as possible after class, fleshing them out while the material still is fresh.

Do not be afraid to ask questions. Often, people hesitate to ask questions because they fear they will appear foolish. In reality, asking good questions is a sign of intelligence; after all, you have to be insightful enough to realize something is unclear. Keep in mind that frequently your classmates have the same questions you do. Good questions not only can help clarify difficult topics, they also increase the depth of your understanding by suggesting relationships between ideas or establishing the impact of concepts. Learn the best time to ask questions. In small classes, sometimes it is possible to ask questions during a lecture. In a larger setting, it may be best to approach your instructor after class or to make an appointment. If you feel really lost, your instructor may be able to recommend a peer tutor or an academic counseling service to help you.

Preparing for and Taking Tests

Tests are an opportunity for you to demonstrate how much you have learned. Many strategies are proven to improve performance on tests. To do your best on a test, follow these guidelines:

Find out as much as you can about the test. Ask your instructor what material will be covered, what types of questions will be used, how much time you will have, and what supplies you will need (pencil or pen, paper or bluebook, calculator, perhaps even notes or a textbook if it is an open-book test).

You will be more likely to do your best work if there are no surprises. Occasionally, copies of previous tests are available. These are invaluable aids in test preparation.

Use your resources wisely. Start studying by reviewing your notes and, in *Microsoft Office 2010: Introductory*, by reviewing the What You Should Know section at the end of each chapter. Review carefully and attempt to anticipate some of the questions that may be asked. Reread sections in your textbook on topics you are not sure of or that seem especially important. Try to really comprehend, and not merely memorize, the material. If you truly understand a concept, you no doubt will be able to answer any question, regardless of the type. Understanding often makes remembering easier. For example, if you know how font size is measured, it is simple to recall the font sizes commonly used in documents and worksheets. When memorizing is necessary, use whatever techniques work best for you (memory tricks, verbal repetition, flash cards, and so on).

Avoid cramming. To prepare for an athletic contest, you would not practice for 12 straight hours before the event. In the same way, you should not expect to do well on a test by spending the entire night before cramming. When you cram, facts become easily confused, and anything you do to keep them straight probably will be remembered only for a short time. It also is difficult to recognize how concepts are related, which can be an important factor in successful test taking. Try to study in increments over a period of time. Use the night before the test to do a general review of the pertinent material, concentrating on what seems most difficult. Then, get a good night's sleep so you are well rested and at your best when it is time for the test.

Take time to look through the test. Arrive early enough at the test site to get properly settled. Listen for any special instructions that might be given. Skim the entire test before you start. Read the directions carefully. You may not need to answer every question in each section, or you may have to answer some questions in a certain way. Determine the worth of each part, the parts you think can be done most quickly, and the parts you believe will take the longest to complete. Use your assessment to budget your time.

Answer the questions you are sure of first. As you work through the test, read each question carefully and answer the easier ones first. If you are not certain of an answer, skip that question for now, ensuring you get the maximum number of "sure" points and guaranteeing less worry about time when dealing later with the more difficult questions. Occasionally, you will find the information you needed to answer one of the questions you skipped can be found elsewhere in the test. Other times, you suddenly will remember what you need to answer a question you skipped as you are dealing with another part of the test.

Use common sense. Most questions have logical answers. While these answers often require specific knowledge, sometimes it is possible to determine a correct answer with a general grasp of the subject matter and a little common sense. When you go back over the test after you are finished, make sure your answers are reasonable. Do not change an answer, however, unless you are sure your first answer was wrong. If incorrect answers are not penalized any more than having no answer at all, it is better to try a logical guess than to leave an answer blank. But, if you are penalized for incorrect answers (for example, if your final score is the number of correct answers minus the number of incorrect answers), you will have to decide whether or not to answer a question you are not sure of based on how confident you are of your guess.

Using this Workbook

The purpose of this Workbook is to further your understanding of the concepts presented in *Microsoft Office 2010: Introductory*. Each Workbook chapter should be completed *after* you have finished the corresponding chapter in the textbook. The Workbook chapters are divided into sections, each of which has a specific purpose:

Overview. This section provides a brief summary of the chapter's content and a Chapter Outline. Use the Overview to recall the general information in the chapter. The Chapter Outline is a partially completed outline of the chapter, along with the page numbers on which important topics can be found in the text. The Chapter Outline is designed not only to help you review the material, but also to assist you in organizing and seeing the relationships between concepts. Complete the Chapter Outline in as much depth as you feel is necessary. Because your completions should be meaningful to you, they may be different from a classmate's. You can refer directly to the textbook as you work through the outline while rereading the chapter, or you can fill in the outline on your own and then use the textbook to check the information you have supplied. When entering the steps necessary to perform a task, think in general, rather than specific, terms. For example, "Type the worksheet title" is a better completion than "Type Dynamite Music Fourth Quarter Sales."

Review. This is a tool you can use to evaluate your mastery of the chapter. The Review consists of several different types of questions: Matching, True/False, Modified True False, Complete the Table, Definitions, Screen Identification, Multiple Choice, Fill in the Blanks, Dialog Box, Sequence, and Short Answer. Try to complete the Review without referring to your textbook or notes. Leave any answer you are unsure of blank or, if you prefer, guess at the answer but indicate you were unsure by placing a question mark (?) after your response. When you have finished the Review, use *Microsoft Office 2010: Introductory* to check your answers. Correct any answers that were incorrect or uncertain. If necessary, ask your instructor to explain any concepts or techniques that still are unclear.

Activities. These are things you can do to reinforce and expand on the concepts presented in each chapter. Expanding on the Make It Right/Apply Your Knowledge/In the Lab extends your work with one of the chapter exercises.

Introduction to Computers

and How to Purchase Computers and Mobile Devices

Overview

This introduction presents basic concepts associated with computers and their use: what a computer is, what a computer does, and how a computer knows what to do. It describes the principal components of a computer, including input devices, the processor, memory, output devices, and storage devices. You discover how system software is different from application software and become acquainted with the purpose of some personal computer application software packages. Computer communications channels, the Internet, the World Wide Web, and computer viruses and other malware are introduced. Finally, you find out how to purchase computers and mobile devices.

Chapter Outline

I. What is a computer? [COM 2]

A computer is ____

____

____

All computers perform the four basic operations of the information processing cycle:

- ____________________ • ____________________
- ____________________ • ____________________

These operations describe the procedures a computer performs to process data into information and store it for future use.

Data is ____

____

Information is ____

____

Computer users (end users or users) are ______________________________

Green computing involves ______________________________

II. How does a computer know what to do? [COM 4]

A computer program (or software) is ______________________________

____

Once the program is stored, the computer executes one instruction after another until the job is complete.

III. The components of a computer [COM 3]

The six primary components of a computer are ____________________

____

A peripheral is ____________________

IV. Personal computers and mobile devices [COM 4]

A personal computer is ____________________

A mobile computer is ____________________

A mobile device is ____________________

A. Desktop computers [COM 4]

A desktop computer is ____________________

B. Notebook computers [COM 4]

A notebook (laptop) computer is ____________________

A netbook is ____________________

The Tablet PC is ____________________

C. Mobile devices [COM 4]

Mobile devices usually store ____________________

A smart phone is ____________________

A portable media player is ____________________

A digital camera is ____________________

V. Input devices [COM 5]

An input device is ____________________

____

The two primary input devices are the keyboard and the mouse.

A. Keyboard [COM 5]

A keyboard is ____________________

____

A stylus is ____________________

B. Mouse and other pointing devices [COM 6]

A mouse is ____________________

____

A mouse is used to control the ____________________

____

A touchpad is ____________________

1. Other input for mobile devices [COM 7]

Most mobile devices use a variety of alternatives for entering data and instructions.

VI. System unit [COM 8]

The system unit is ______________________________

The motherboard (system board) is ______________________________

A. Processor [COM 8]

The processor (central processing unit or CPU) interprets and carries out ______________________________

____

The processor contains a control unit and an arithmetic/logic unit.

The control unit directs and coordinates ______________________________

The arithmetic/logic unit performs ______________________________

B. Memory [COM 8]

Memory (random access memory or RAM) consists of ______________________________

____

The amount of memory typically is measured in kilobytes, megabytes, gigabytes, or terabytes.

One kilobyte (K or KB) equals ______________________________

One megabyte (MB) equals ______________________________

One gigabyte (GB) equals ______________________________

One terabyte (TB) equals ______________________________

VII. Output devices [COM 9]

Output devices make ______________________________

____

Two commonly used output devices are printers and display devices.

A. Printers [COM 9]

A photo printer produces ______________________________

____

A multifunctional peripheral (or all-in-one device) is ______________________________

____

B. Display devices [COM 10]

A display device is ______________________________

____

A monitor is ______________________________

____

An LCD monitor uses ______________________________

Pixels are ______________________________

Resolution is ______________________________

VIII. Storage devices [COM 10]

A storage device is ______________________________

____

A storage medium is ______________________________

A. Hard disks [COM 11]

A hard disk is ______________________________

____

A track is ______________________________

Sectors are ______________________________

A head crash occurs ______________________________

A backup is ______________________________

1. Portable hard disks [COM 12]

An external hard disk is ______________________________

____

A removable hard disk is ______________________________

____

2. Flash memory storage [COM 12]

Solid state media consist entirely of ______________________________

____

A solid state drive (SSD) is ______________________________

____

A memory card is ______________________________

____

A USB flash (thumb) drive is ______________________________

____

An ExpressCard module is ______________________________

____

B. Optical discs [COM 15]

An optical disc is ______________________________

____

A CD-ROM (compact disc – read-only memory) is ______________________________

____

To read a CD-ROM, insert the disc in a CD-ROM drive or a CD-ROM player.

A CD-R (compact disc – recordable) is ______________________________

____

A CD-RW (compact disc – rewriteable) is ______________________________

____

A DVD-ROM (digital video disc – ROM) is ______________________________

____

To read a DVD-ROM, you need a DVD-ROM drive or DVD player.

Blu-ray (BD) has ______________________________

DVD-RW, DVD+RW, and DVD+RAM are ______________________________

BD-RE is ______________________________

C. Cloud storage [COM 17]

Cloud storage is ______________________________

____

IX. Communications devices [COM 17]

A communications device is ______________________________

____

Communications occur over ______________________________

X. Computer software [COM 18]

Software (or programs) consists of ______________________________

A graphical user interface (GUI) allows you to ______________________________

Installing is ______________________________

Uninstalling is ______________________________

A Web application is ______________________________

Two types of software are system software and application software.

A. System software [COM 18]

System software consists of ______________________________

____

The operating system coordinates ______________________________

____

A utility program allows ______________________________

B. Application software [COM 18]

Application software consists of ______________________________

____

Commonly used applications include word processing, presentation, spreadsheet, database, and e-mail.

1. Word processing [COM 19]

   Word processing software is ______________________________

   ____

2. Presentation [COM 19]

   Presentation software allows ______________________________

   ____

3. Spreadsheet [COM 20]

   Spreadsheet software allows ______________________________

   ____

   A worksheet is ______________________________

4. Database [COM 20]

   A database is ______________________________

   Database software allows ______________________________

   ____

5. E-mail [COM 21]

   An e-mail program is used to ______________________________

   ____

XI. Networks and the Internet [COM 21]

A network is ______________________________

____

When a computer is online, it is ______________________________

A local area network (LAN) is ______________________________

____

A wireless LAN (WLAN) is ______________________________

____

A wide area network (WAN) is ______________________________

____

A. The Internet [COM 22]

The Internet is ______________________________

____

More than one billion people around the world use the Internet to:

- ______________________________
- ______________________________
- ______________________________
- ______________________________
- ______________________________

An access provider is ______________________________

An Internet service provider (ISP) is ______________________________

____

An online service provider (OSP) provides ______________________________

____

A wireless Internet service provider (wireless data provider) is ______________________________

____

B. The World Wide Web [COM 24]

The World Wide Web (or the Web) is ______________________________

____

A Web page is ______________________________

____

A Web site is ______________________________

A Web browser is ______________________________

A Web page has a unique address, called a(n) ______________________________

http:// stands for ______________________________

A Web server is ______________________________

The term Web 2.0 refers to ______________________________

A social networking Web site (or online social network) is ______________________________

____

A blog is ______________________________

E-commerce (electronic commerce) is ______________________________

____

C. Searching the Web [COM 25]

A search engine is ______________________________

____

Search text describes ______________________________

____

A subject directory classifies ______________________________

XII. Computer viruses and other malware [COM 26]

A virus is ______________________________

A worm is ______________________________

A Trojan horse is ______________________________

A rootkit is ______________________________

Malware is ____

An antivirus program protects ____

XIII. Buyer's Guide: How to purchase computers and mobile devices [COM 27]

A. How to purchase a desktop computer [COM 28]

Considerations for purchasing a desktop computer:

1. ____
2. ____
3. ____
4. ____
5. ____
6. ____
7. ____
8. ____
9. ____
10. ____
11. ____
12. ____
13. ____
14. ____
15. ____

B. How to purchase a notebook computer [COM 32]

Considerations for purchasing a notebook computer:

1. ____
2. ____
3. ____
4. ____
5. ____
6. ____
7. ____
8. ____
9. ____
10. ____
11. ____
12. ____
13. ____

14. __________

15. __________

16. __________

C. How to purchase a smart phone [COM 35]

Considerations for purchasing a smart phone:

1. __________
2. __________
3. __________
4. __________
5. __________
6. __________
7. __________

D. How to purchase a portable media player [COM 36]

Considerations for purchasing a portable media player:

1. __________
2. __________
3. __________
4. __________
5. __________
6. __________
7. __________
8. __________

E. How to purchase a digital camera [COM 37]

Considerations for purchasing a digital camera:

1. __________
2. __________
3. __________
4. __________
5. __________
6. __________
7. __________
8. __________
9. __________
10. __________

Review

Matching (5)

Match each term on the left with the best description from the right.

___ 1. input device

___ 2. processor

___ 3. memory

___ 4. output device

___ 5. storage device

a. makes the information resulting from processing available for use

b. stores instructions and data while they are not being processed

c. converts a computer's digital signals into analog signals that can be sent over telephone lines

d. interprets and carries out the basic instructions that operate a computer

e. stores data — including numbers, letters, graphics, and sound — while it is being processed

f. links a limited geographical area, such as a school computer laboratory or group of buildings

g. allows data, programs, commands, and user responses to be entered into a computer

True-False (5)

*Circle **T** if the statement is true and **F** if the statement is false.*

T F 1. All computer processing requires data.

T F 2. The control unit performs the logical and arithmetic processes.

T F 3. A computer with 512 MB of memory can hold about 512 million characters.

T F 4. Generally, the more expensive the laser printer, the more pages it can print per minute.

T F 5. Dimensionality is the number of horizontal and vertical pixels in a display device.

Modified True-False (5)

*Circle **T** if the statement is true. If the statement is false, circle **F** and make the statement true by writing the replacement for the underlined word or phrase in the blank.*

T F 1. A(n) <u>sector</u> is a narrow recording band that forms a full circle on the surface of the disk.

____

T F 2. You <u>can</u> erase the contents of CD-ROMs.

____

T F 3. Some widely used <u>operating</u> system software includes Web page authoring, personal finance, project management, accounting, computer-aided design, and desktop publishing.

____

T F 4. <u>Access</u> providers are categorized as ISPs, online service providers, and wireless Internet service providers.

____

T F 5. When you buy a computer system, use <u>cash</u> to purchase your system.

____

Definitions (5)

Briefly define each term.

1. computer user ______________________________
2. processor ______________________________
3. URL ______________________________
4. http:// ______________________________
5. e-commerce ______________________________

Personal Computer Devices (10)

Identify the devices that constitute the personal computer in Figure COM1, and note the operation(s) in the information processing cycle for which they are used.

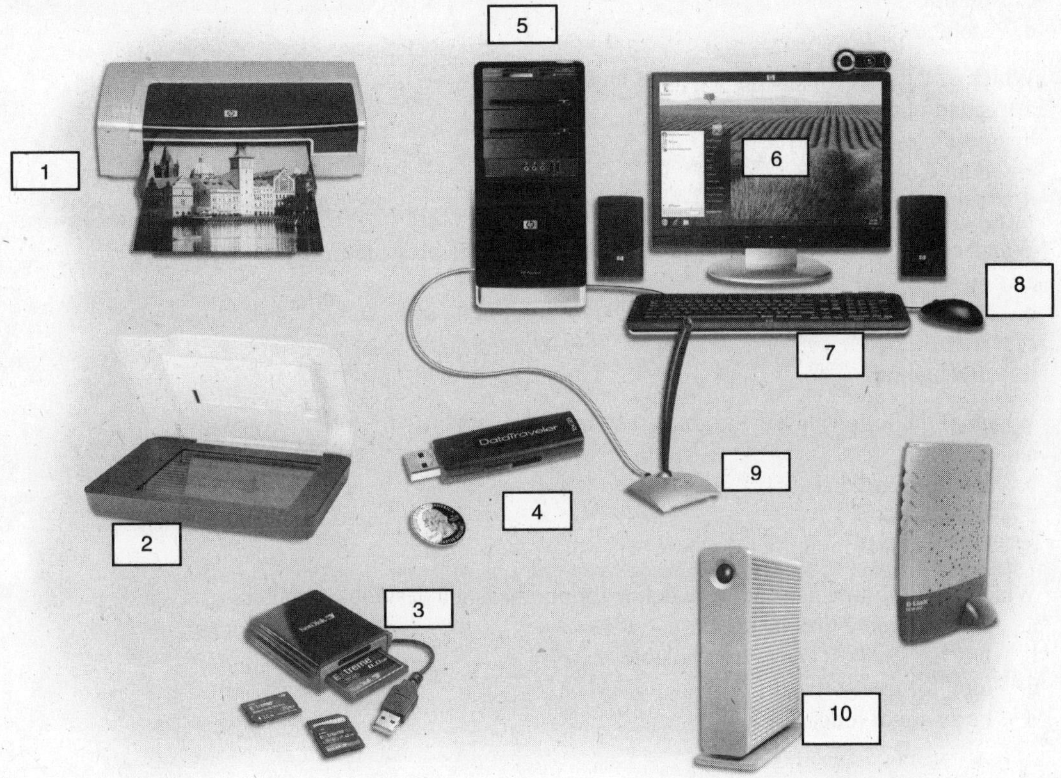

Figure COM1

	Device	**Information Processing Operation(s)**
1.	______________	______________________________
2.	______________	______________________________
3.	______________	______________________________
4.	______________	______________________________

5. ____________________ ____

6. ____________________ ____

7. ____________________ ____

8. ____________________ ____

9. ____________________ ____

10. ____________________ ____

Multiple Choice (5)

Circle the letter of the best answer.

1. During what operation in the information processing cycle is the information created put into some form, such as a printed report or color graphics?
   a. input
   b. process
   c. output
   d. storage

2. Which of the following is not a type of mobile device?
   a. smart phone
   b. portable media player
   c. digital camera
   d. Tablet PC

3. Which of the following looks like a tiny ink pen but uses pressure instead of ink?
   a. digital pencil
   b. trackpad
   c. stylus
   d. touchpoint

4. Which of the following has the greatest storage capacity?
   a. SSD
   b. internal hard disks
   c. CD-ROMs
   d. DVD-ROMs

5. Which of the following is not a guideline for purchasing a desktop computer?
   a. consider more than just price
   b. buy the smallest computer available
   c. look for free software
   d. be aware of hidden costs

Understanding a URL (4)

Identify the numbered parts of the URL in Figure COM2.

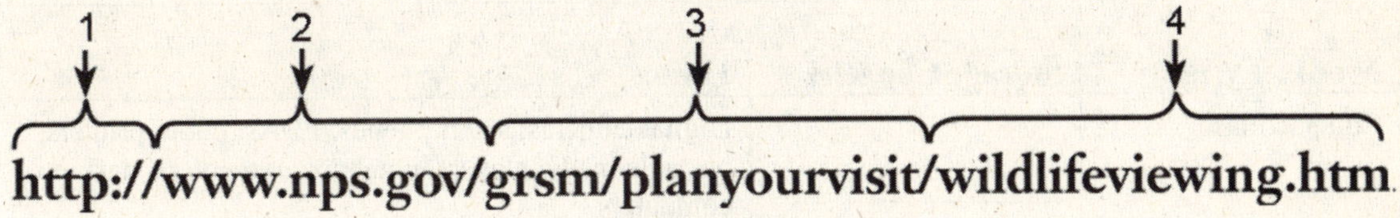

Figure COM2

1. ______________________________
2. ______________________________
3. ______________________________
4. ______________________________

Fill in the Blanks (5)

Write a word (or words) in the blank to complete each sentence correctly.

1. The surface of the screen of an LCD monitor is composed of individual picture elements called ______________________.
2. A(n) ______________________ is a duplicate of a file, program, or disk placed on a separate storage medium that you can use in case the original is lost, damaged, or destroyed.
3. A Web ______________________ is a computer that delivers requested Web pages.
4. A(n) ______________________ is a program that finds Web sites, Web pages, images, videos, news, maps, and other information related to a specific topic.
5. A(n) ______________________ is a collection of data organized in a manner that allows access, retrieval, and use of that data.

Sequence (4)

Use the numbers 1 – 4 to place these items in order.

___ When software requests a disk access, the read/write heads determine the current or new location of the data.

___ The head actuator positions the read/write head arms over the correct location on the platters to read or write data.

___ The circuit board controls the movement of the head actuator and a small motor.

___ A small motor spins the platters while the computer is running.

Complete the Table

VARIOUS MEMORY CARDS

Media Type	Storage Capacity	Use
CompactFlash	____________	Digital cameras, smart phones, PDAs, photo printers, portable media players, notebook computers, desktop computers
Secure Digital	512 MB to 8 GB	____________ ____________
____________	4 to 32 GB	Digital cameras
MicroSD	1 to 2 GB	____________ ____________ ____________ ____________
Memory Stick PRO Duo	1 to 16 GB	____________ ____________

Short Answer (5)

Write a brief answer to each question.

1. What are four steps for preventing viruses and other malware?

2. How does an LCD monitor work?

3. How is system software different from application software? Why is a graphical user interface (GUI) important?

4. Why do people use the Internet? What are the three ways in which users connect to the Internet?

5. What is cloud storage? What are three different types of cloud storage?

Activities

Expanding on the Case

Perform the following tasks.

Expand on the report written in Case Study 2 by interviewing the representative of a business (e.g., a travel agency, a small local bookseller) that has been negatively impacted by the Internet.

or

Interview a classmate about his or her ideal notebook computer, as discussed in Case Study 3, and write the list of the hardware and software that would be included, the cost of each item, the total cost for the entire system, and his or her main reasons for using this system.

Office 2010 and Windows 7: Essential Concepts and Skills

Overview

This chapter illustrates the Windows 7 interface. After starting Windows 7, you learn the components of the desktop and several mouse operations. You open, close, move, resize, minimize, maximize, and scroll a window. You use folder windows to expand and collapse drives and folders, display drive and folder contents, create folders, and rename and then delete a file. You also learn some basic features of some Microsoft Office 2010 programs, including Word, PowerPoint, Excel, and Access. You discover the common elements that exist among these different Office programs. You learn how to save basic document, presentation, spreadsheet, and database files, and you learn about additional Office programs, including Outlook, Publisher, and OneNote. Finally, you learn about Microsoft Office Help and how to use the Office Help window, you are introduced to the Windows 7 Help and Support Center, and you learn how to use it to obtain more information about Windows 7.

Chapter Outline

I. Office 2010 and Windows 7 [OFF 2]

A. Overview [OFF 2]

II. Introduction to the Windows 7 operating system [OFF 2]

Windows 7 is ____

____

An operating system is ____

Application software consists of ____

____

A. Using a mouse [OFF 2]

Windows users work with a mouse that has at least two buttons.

B. Scrolling [OFF 4]

A scroll bar is ____

____

A scroll bar contains ____

____

C. Shortcut keys [OFF 4]

A shortcut key (or keyboard shortcut) is ____________________

____

D. Starting Windows 7 [OFF 5]

A user account identifies ____________________

____

A user name is ____________________

A password is ____________________

____

A user icon is ____________________

Logging on opens ____________________

The Welcome screen shows ____________________

The Restart command closes ____________________

The Sleep command waits for ____________________

The Shut down command is used to ____________________

☞ To log on to the computer

1. ____________________

____

2. ____________________

E. The Windows 7 desktop [OFF 7]

The Recycle Bin is ____________________

____

III. Introduction to Microsoft Office 2010 [OFF 7]

Microsoft Office 2010 is ____________________

____

A. Microsoft Office 2010 programs [OFF 8]

Microsoft Word 2010 is ____________________

Microsoft PowerPoint 2010 is ____________________

Microsoft Excel 2010 is ____________________

Microsoft Access 2010 is ____________________

Microsoft Outlook 2010 is ____________________

Microsoft Publisher 2010 is ____________________

Microsoft OneNote 2010 is ____________________

Microsoft InfoPath 2010 is ____________________

Microsoft SharePoint Workspace 2010 is ____________________

Microsoft Communicator is ______________________________

Microsoft Web Apps is ______________________________

B. Microsoft Office 2010 suites [OFF 8]

A suite is ______________________________

Microsoft Office programs use common dialog boxes for ______________________________

____

IV. Starting and using a program [OFF 9]

A. Word [OFF 9]

☞ To start a program using the Start menu

The Start button is used to ______________________________

A folder is ______________________________

The Start menu allows you to ______________________________

____

A menu is ______________________________

A command performs ______________________________

1. ______________________________

2. ______________________________

A pane is ______________________________

3. ______________________________

4. ______________________________

A window is ______________________________

A title bar is ______________________________

☞ To maximize a window

To maximize a window means to ______________________________

1. ______________________________

____

B. The Word document window, Ribbon, and elements common to Office programs [OFF 12]

A document window is used to ______________________________

The default (preset) view is ______________________________

1. Scroll bars [OFF 12]

You use a scroll bar to display different portions of a document in the document window.

2. Status bar [OFF 13]

The status bar presents ______________________________

3. Ribbon [OFF 14]

The Ribbon is ______________________________

Each tab contains ______________________________

The Home tab contains ______________________________

Tool tabs display when ______________________________

A gallery is ______________________________

Live preview is ______________________________

An Enhanced ScreenTip is ______________________________

A Dialog Box Launcher displays ______________________________

A task pane is ______________________________

4. Mini toolbar [OFF 15]

   The Mini toolbar contains ______________________________

   ____

5. Quick Access Toolbar [OFF 16]

   The Quick Access Toolbar provides ______________________________

   ____

6. KeyTips [OFF 16]

   KeyTips are used to ______________________________

   ____

☞ To display a different tab on the Ribbon

The active tab is ______________________________

1. ______________________________

   ____

☞ To minimize, display, and restore the Ribbon

1. ______________________________
2. ______________________________
3. ______________________________

   ____

☞ To display and use a shortcut menu

A shortcut menu is ______________________________

1. ______________________________
2. ______________________________
3. ______________________________
4. ______________________________

☞ To customize the Quick Access Toolbar

1. ______________________________
2. ______________________________

☞ To enter text in a document

1. ______________________________

2. ______________________________

V. Saving and organizing files [OFF 21]

A file name is ______________________________

A. Organizing files and folders [OFF 21]

A path consists of ______________________________

____

☞ To create a folder

1. ______________________________

2. ______________________________

3. ______________________________

____

____

B. Folder windows [OFF 24]

Most users rely on folder windows for ______________________________

____

The Address bar provides ______________________________

The Previous Locations button saves ______________________________

The Refresh button refreshes ______________________________

The search box contains ______________________________

A shortcut is ______________________________

The Command bar contains ______________________________

The navigation pane contains ______________________________

The Favorites area contains ______________________________

The Libraries area shows ______________________________

A library helps you ______________________________

☞ To create a folder within a folder

1. ______________________________

2. ______________________________

____

____

☞ To expand a folder, scroll through folder contents, and collapse a folder

1. ______________________________

____

____

____

2. ______________________________

☞ To switch from one program to another

1. ______________________________

2. ______________________________

☞ To save a file in a folder

1. ______________________________

2. ______________________________

3. ______________________________

____

____

____

____

____

4. ______________________________

C. Navigating in dialog boxes [OFF 30]

Navigating is ______________________________

____

☞ To minimize and restore a window

A minimized window is ______________________________

1. ______________________________

____

2. ______________________________

3. ______________________________

D. Screen resolution [OFF 31]

Screen resolution indicates ______________________________

____

☞ To change the screen resolution

1. ______________________________

____

2. ______________________________

3. ______________________________

A slider is ______________________________

4. ______________________________

5.

☞ To quit an Office program with one document open

1.

2.

The Backstage view contains

3.

VI. Additional Microsoft Office programs [OFF 36]

A. PowerPoint [OFF 36]

A PowerPoint presentation is also called a(n)

Additional PowerPoint features include the following:

Word processing:

Outlining:

Charting:

Drawing:

Inserting multimedia:

Saving to the Web:

E-mailing:

Collaborating:

Preparing delivery:

☞ To start a program using the search box

1.

2.

3.

B. The PowerPoint window and Ribbon [OFF 39]

A slide is

Layouts are

The default layout is

Landscape orientation is

1. Placeholders [OFF 39]

Placeholders are

2. Ribbon [OFF 40]

The Ribbon in PowerPoint is similar to the one in other Microsoft Office programs.

☞ To enter content in a title slide

1. ______________________________

2. ______________________________

☞ To create a new Office document from the Backstage view

1. ______________________________

The File tab is used ______________________________

2. ______________________________

3. ______________________________

☞ To close an Office file using the Backstage view

1. ______________________________

2. ______________________________

☞ To open a recent Office file using the Backstage view

1. ______________________________

____

2. ______________________________

C. Excel [OFF 46]

The four major parts of Excel are:

______________ ______________

______________ ______________

A workbook is ______________________________

A worksheet is ______________________________

☞ To create a new blank Office document from Windows Explorer

1. ______________________________

____

____

____

____

2. ______________________________

3. ______________________________

☞ To start a program from Windows Explorer and open a file

1. ______________________________

____

2. ______________________________________

____

____

D. Unique features of Excel [OFF 49]

A sheet tab contains ______________________________________

1. The worksheet [OFF 49]

The column heading identifies ______________________________________

The row heading identifies ______________________________________

A cell is ______________________________________

A cell reference is ______________________________________

The active cell is ______________________________________

Gridlines are ______________________________________

2. Ribbon [OFF 49]

When you start Excel, the Ribbon displays eight main tabs: File, Home, Insert, Page Layout, Formulas, Data, Review, and View.

3. Formula bar [OFF 50]

The formula bar displays ______________________________________

The Name box displays ______________________________________

☞ To enter a worksheet title

Text is ______________________________________

1. ______________________________________

2. ______________________________________

3. ______________________________________

☞ To save an existing Office document with the same file name

1. ______________________________________

E. Access [OFF 53]

A database is ______________________________________

Microsoft Access 2010 (Access) is ______________________________________

A database management system is ______________________________________

F. Unique elements of Access [OFF 54]

The Access work area is ______________________________________

Object tabs appear ______________________________________

1. Ribbon [OFF 54]

☞ To create an Access database

1. ______________________________

____

____

2. ______________________________

____

3. ______________________________

4. ______________________________

☞ To open an existing Office file

1. ______________________________

____

2. ______________________________

3. ______________________________

4. ______________________________

VII. Other Office programs [OFF 58]

A. Outlook [OFF 58]

Outlook is ______________________________

Electronic mail (e-mail) is ______________________________

1. The Outlook window [OFF 58]

The Outlook window is divided into six panes: the Favorites folder pane, the Mail folder pane, the Navigation pane on the left, the Inbox message pane to the left of center, the Reading pane to the right of center, and the People pane just below the Reading Pane.

B. Publisher [OFF 59]

Publisher is ______________________________

1. The Publisher window [OFF 60]

Publication types are ______________________________

C. OneNote [OFF 61]

OneNote is ______________________________

1. The OneNote window [OFF 62]

The notebook is ______________________________

Pages are ______________________________

Pages are grouped into ______________________________

Folders are ______________________________

VIII. Moving, renaming, and deleting files [OFF 62]

File management is ______________________________

☞ To rename a file

1. ______________________________

____

____

2. ______________________________

☞ To move a file

1. ______________________________

____

____

☞ To delete a file

1. ______________________________

____

____

2. ______________________________

____

IX. Microsoft Office and Windows Help [OFF 66]

☞ To open the Help window in an Office program

1. ______________________________

____

A. Moving and resizing windows [OFF 66]

☞ To move a window by dragging

1. ______________________________

☞ To resize a window by dragging

1. ______________________________

____

B. Using Office Help [OFF 68]

You can search for help by using any of three methods:

1. ______________________________

2. ______________________________

3. ______________________________

☞ To obtain help using the 'Type words to search for' text box

1. ______________________________

____

____

2. ______________________________

3. ______________________________

4. ______________________________

☞ To obtain help using the help links

1. ______________________________

☞ To obtain help using the Table of Contents

1. ______________________________

____

2. ______________________________

____

____

____

X. Obtaining help while working in an Office program [OFF 72]

A. Using Windows Help and Support [OFF 73]

☞ To start Windows Help and Support

1. ______________________________

2. ______________________________

____

Review

Matching (5)

Match each term on the left with the correct example from the right.

___ 1. Right-click

___ 2. Triple-click

___ 3. Press wheel

___ 4. Drag

___ 5. Click

a. select or deselect items on the screen or start a program or program feature

b. move an object from one location to another

c. scroll continuously

d. select a paragraph

e. display a shortcut menu

f. scroll horizontally (left and right)

g. position the pointer on the screen

True-False (5)

*Circle **T** if the statement is true and **F** if the statement is false.*

T F 1. By default, a collapsed folder lists the folders it contains.

T F 2. From the Backstage view in PowerPoint, you can create, open, print, and save presentations.

T F 3. Text is used to place titles on the worksheet.

T F 4. Publisher is a note-taking program that assists you in entering, saving, organizing, searching, and using notes.

T F 5. Windows Help and Support is available when using any Microsoft program running under Windows 7.

Modified True-False (5)

*Circle **T** if the statement is true. If the statement is false, circle **F** and make the statement true by writing the replacement for the underlined word or phrase in the blank.*

T F 1. The top of a window has a(n) <u>name</u> bar, which is horizontal space that contains the window's name.

____

T F 2. A(n) <u>dialog box</u> is a window that can remain open and visible while you work in the document.

____

T F 3. When you start a program in Windows 7, it appears on the <u>desktop</u>.

____

T F 4. The <u>Address</u> bar contains five buttons used to accomplish various tasks related to organizing and managing the contents of the open window.

____

T F 5. When you <u>increase</u> the screen resolution, Windows displays more information on the screen, but the information decreases in size.

____

Definitions (5)

Briefly define each term.

1. operating system ______________________
2. software ______________________
3. password ______________________
4. workbook ______________________
5. database ______________________

The Windows 7 Desktop (5)

Identify the elements indicated in Figure OFF1.

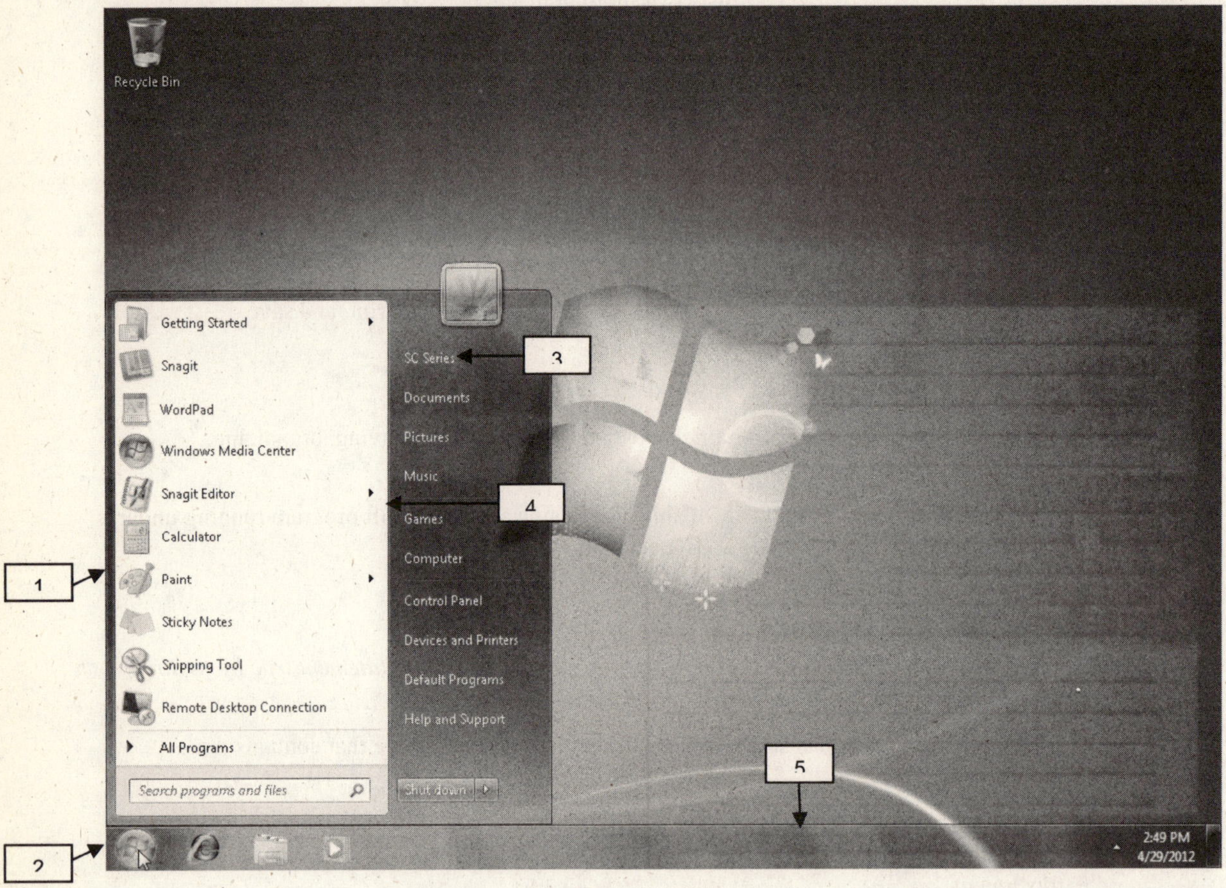

Figure OFF1

1. ______________________
2. ______________________
3. ______________________
4. ______________________
5. ______________________

Multiple Choice (5)

Circle the letter of the best answer.

1. Which of the following commands is not available on the Shut down options button?
   a. Reboot
   b. Restart
   c. Sleep
   d. Shut down
2. Which of the following is not a Microsoft Office 2010 program?
   a. Microsoft InfoPath 2010
   b. Microsoft Web Apps
   c. Microsoft Communicator
   d. Microsoft Firefox 2010
3. Which of the following is not available in Microsoft Office Standard 2010 edition?
   a. Outlook
   b. Access
   c. Publisher
   d. OneNote
4. Which of the following tabs do all Office programs have?
   a. Command
   b. Options
   c. Home
   d. Tools
5. What is the basic unit of a PowerPoint presentation?
   a. path
   b. title
   c. slide
   d. icon

The Folders List in Windows 7 (5)

Answer the following questions about the window shown in Figure OFF2.

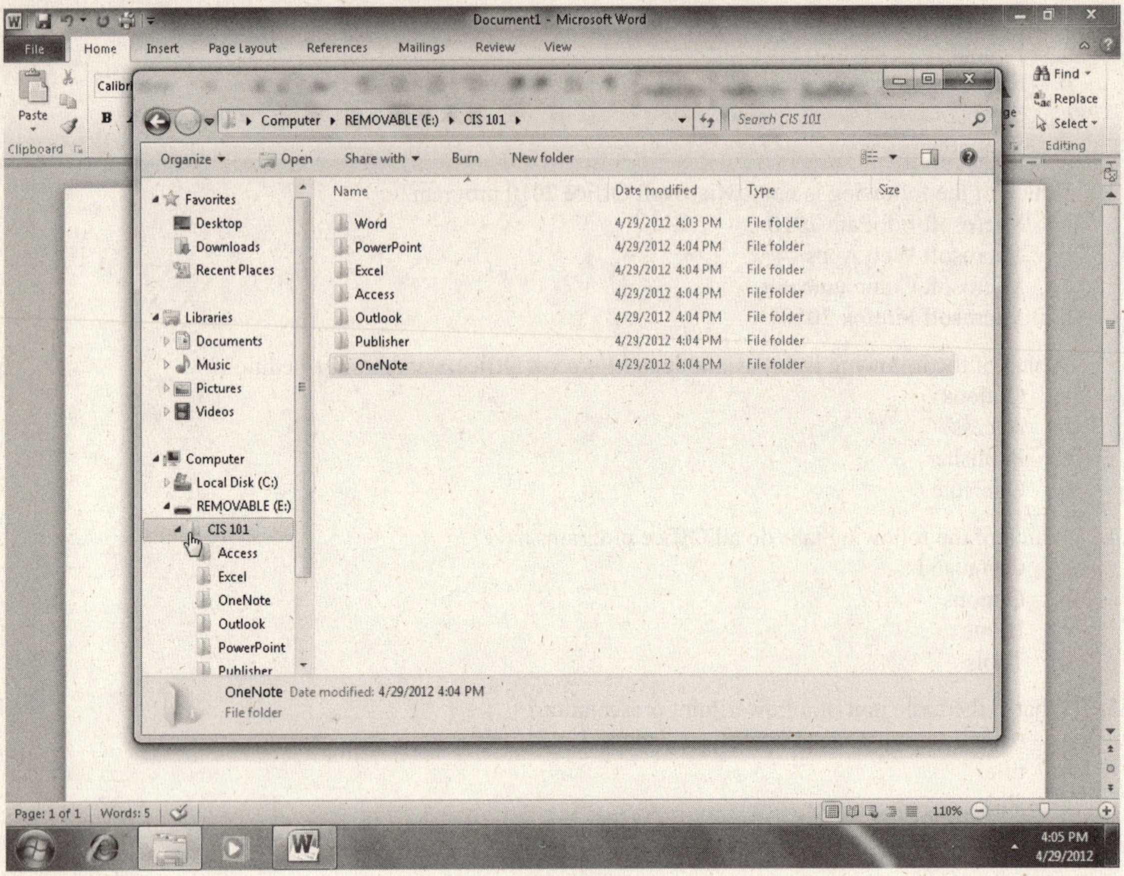

Figure OFF2

1. Why are the folders indented below the CIS 101 folder? ______________________________

   ____

2. What does an expanded folder display? ______________________________

3. What do the white arrows indicate? ______________________________

4. What do the black arrows indicate? ______________________________

5. Why is there a scroll bar in the navigation pane? ______________________________

Fill in the Blanks (5)

Write a word (or words) in the blank to complete each sentence correctly.

1. A(n) ______________________ consists of a drive letter (preceded by a drive name when necessary) and colon, to identify the storage device, and one or more folder names.

2. The ______________________ bar in a folder window provides quick navigation options.

3. A(n) ________________________ is another name for a PowerPoint presentation.
4. The horizontal and vertical lines on an Excel worksheet are called ________________________.
5. ________________________ is the transmission of messages and files over a computer network.

Sequence (5)

Use the numbers 1 – 5 to show the order in which these steps should be performed to change the screen resolution.

___ Click the Resolution button to display the resolution slider.

___ Click Screen resolution on the shortcut menu.

___ Drag the resolution slider until the desired screen resolution is selected.

___ Right-click an empty area on the desktop.

___ Click an empty area of the Screen resolution window, click the OK button to change the screen resolution and display the Display Settings dialog box, and click the Keep changes button.

Complete the Table

MOUSE OPERATIONS

Operation	Mouse Action
________________________	Move the mouse until the pointer on the desktop is positioned on the item of choice.
________________________	Point and release the secondary mouse button, which usually is the right mouse button.
________________________	Quickly press and release the left mouse button three times without moving the mouse.
________________________	Point to an item, hold down the right mouse button, move the item to the desired location on the screen, and then release the right mouse button.
________________________	Press the wheel toward the right or left.

Short Answer (5)

Write a brief answer to each question.

1. What is displayed on the desktop when you log on to the computer?

2. What are the four major parts of Excel?

3. What is a shortcut menu?

4. Should you keep the Folders list expanded or collapsed?

5. What are the three methods of searching for help from the Help window?

Activities

Expanding on the Lab

Perform the following tasks.

1. Connect the USB flash drive that you used for In the Lab 2 to an available USB port and then open the USB flash drive window.
2. Display the contents of the Pete's Pet Supplies folder.
3. Change the name of the Fish folder to **Aquatic**.
4. Within the Aquatic folder, create two additional folders: one for **Fish** and the second for **Crustaceans**.
5. Within the Dogs folder, create two additional folders: one for **Pure Breeds** and the second for **Mixed Breeds**.
6. Create a Word document containing the following lines of text

   Golden Retriever
   German Shepherd
   Poodle

   and then save it in the Pure Breeds folder.
7. Right-click the Cats folder and click Properties on the shortcut menu to display the properties of the folder. List all of the properties that you see.
8. Click the Cancel button in the Properties dialog box. Close all open windows.

Microsoft Word 2010

Chapter One
Creating, Formatting, and Editing a Word Document with Pictures

Overview

This chapter introduces entering text in a document, formatting text, inserting a picture, formatting a picture, adding a page border, and printing a document.

Chapter Outline

I. Introduction [WD 2]

II. Project — Flyer with Pictures [WD 2]

Examples of how you can format text include ______________________________

☞ To start Word

1. ______________________________
2. ______________________________
3. ______________________________
4. ______________________________
5. ______________________________
6. ______________________________

III. Entering text [WD 5]

The headline is ______________________________

The body copy consists of ______________________________

The signature line contains ______________________________

☞ To type text

1. ______________________________

The Spelling and Grammar Check icon appears when ______________________________

____

2. ______________________________

____

☞ To display formatting marks

A formatting mark (nonprinting character) is ______________________

____

1. ______________________

☞ To insert a blank line

1. ______________________

A. Wordwrap [WD 8]

Wordwrap allows you to ______________________

____

☞ To wordwrap text as you type

1. ______________________

____

B. Spelling and Grammar Check [WD 9]

As you type text in a document, Word checks your typing for ______________________

____

☞ To check spelling and grammar as you type

1. ______________________

2. ______________________

____

3. ______________________

____

C. Navigating a document [WD 11]

You view only a portion of a document on the screen through the document window.

IV. Formatting paragraphs and characters [WD 12]

To format a document means to ______________________

Paragraph formatting is ______________________

____

Character formatting is ______________________

____

The font (typeface) defines ______________________

____

Font size specifies ______________________

A single point is ______________________

A theme is ______________________________

A left-aligned paragraph is ______________________________

☞ To center a paragraph

1. ______________________________

____

2. ______________________________

A. Formatting single versus multiple paragraphs and characters [WD 15]

To format multiple paragraphs or words, you must first ______________________________

____

☞ To select a line

1. ______________________________

____

2. ______________________________

____

☞ To change the font size of selected text

1. ______________________________

____

2. ______________________________

3. ______________________________

☞ To change the font of selected text

1. ______________________________

2. ______________________________

____

3. ______________________________

☞ To change the case of selected text

1. ______________________________

2. ______________________________

☞ To apply a text effect to selected text

1. ______________________________

2. ______________________________

3. ______________________________

4. ______________________________

☞ To shade a paragraph

When you shade text, Word ______________________________

1. ______________________________

____

2. ______________________________

3. ______________________________

☞ To select multiple lines

1. ______________________________

____

2. ______________________________

☞ To bullet a list of paragraphs

A bulleted list is ______________________________

1. ______________________________

____

2. ______________________________

☞ To undo and redo an action

1. ______________________________

____

2. ______________________________

____

☞ To italicize text

Italicized text has ______________________________

1. ______________________________

____

☞ To color text

1. ______________________________

2. ______________________________

3. ______________________________

☞ To use the Mini toolbar to format text

1. ______________________________

2. ______________________________

3. ______________________________

4. ______________________________

5. ______________________________

☞ To select a group of words

1. ______________________________

____

2. ______________________________

☞ To underline text

Underlined text prints ______

1. ______

______

☞ To bold text

Bold characters appear ______

1. ______

2. ______

☞ To change theme colors

A color scheme is ______

1. ______

2. ______

B. Selecting text [WD 30]

Table 1-3 summarizes the techniques used to select various items.

V. Inserting and formatting pictures in a Word document [WD 30]

To download a picture means ______

______

A virus is ______

☞ To insert a picture

1. ______

______

______

2. ______

______

______

______

3. ______

A selection rectangle surrounds ______

Sizing handles are ______

☞ To zoom the document

1. ______

______

☞ To resize a graphic

Resizing includes ______

1. ______

2. ____________________

3. ____________________

4. ____________________

☞ To resize a graphic by entering exact measurements

1. ____________________

2. ____________________

☞ To apply a picture style

A style is ____________________

1. ____________________

2. ____________________

____

3. ____________________

☞ To apply picture effects

1. ____________________

2. ____________________

3. ____________________

4. ____________________

VI. Enhancing the page [WD 40]

☞ To view one page

1. ____________________

2. ____________________

☞ To add a page border

1. ____________________

____

2. ____________________

____

3. ____________________

____

4. ____________________

☞ To change spacing before and after a paragraph

1. ____________________

____

2. ____________________

____

VII. Correcting errors and revising a document [WD 44]

Changes to a document can be required because the document contains an error or because of new circumstances.

A. Types of changes made to documents [WD 44]

1. Additions [WD 44]

____

2. Deletions [WD 44]

____

3. Modifications [WD 44]

____

☞ To insert text in an existing document

1. ______________________________

2. ______________________________

In insert mode, as you type a character ______________________________

____

B. Deleting text from an existing document [WD 47]

☞ To delete text

1. ______________________________

2. ______________________________

☞ To move text

With drag-and-drop editing, you select ______________________________

____

1. ______________________________

____

2. ______________________________

3. ______________________________

VIII. Changing document properties [WD 49]

Document properties (metadata) are ______________________________

A keyword is ______________________________

Standard properties are ______________________________

Automatically updated properties include ______________________________

____

☞ To change document properties

The Document Information Panel contains ______________________

1. ______________________

____

2. ______________________

3. ______________________

4. ______________________

____

5. ______________________

☞ To save an existing document with the same file name

1. ______________________

____

IX. Printing a document [WD 51]

A hard copy (printout) is ______________________

Printed copies of your document can be useful for the following reasons:

- ______________________
- ______________________

Green computing involves ______________________

☞ To print a document

1. ______________________

____

2. ______________________

____

3. ______________________

☞ To quit Word

1. ______________________

2. ______________________

Review

Matching (5)

Match each item to select on the left with the appropriate keyboard technique from the right.

___ 1. character(s)	a.	CTRL+SHIFT+RIGHT ARROW (or LEFT ARROW) repeatedly
___ 2. document	b.	CTRL+SHIFT+RIGHT ARROW (or LEFT ARROW)
___ 3. lines	c.	CTRL+SHIFT+DOWN ARROW (or UP ARROW) repeatedly
___ 4. paragraphs	d.	CTRL+SHIFT+DOWN ARROW (or UP ARROW)
___ 5. words	e.	HOME, then SHIFT+DOWN ARROW or END, then SHIFT+UP ARROW
	f.	CTRL+A
	g.	SHIFT+RIGHT ARROW or SHIFT+LEFT ARROW

True-False (5)

*Circle **T** if the statement is true and **F** if the statement is false.*

T F 1. Depending on your computer's resolution, Word may change how the groups and buttons appear on the Ribbon.

T F 2. A blue wavy line indicates the text may be incorrect grammatically.

T F 3. In Word, you cannot select items unless they are adjacent.

T F 4. When the Mini toolbar appears, it is initially transparent.

T F 5. Word includes a collection of predefined graphical images that you can insert in a document.

Modified True-False (5)

*Circle **T** if the statement is true. If the statement is <u>false</u>, circle **F** and make the statement true by writing the replacement for the underlined word or phrase in the blank.*

T F 1. The <u>headline</u> highlights the key points of a message in as few words as possible.

____

T F 2. Adding bullets to paragraphs is an example of <u>character</u> formatting.

____

T F 3. A color scheme in Word is a document theme that identifies <u>six</u> complementary colors for text, background, accents, and links in a document.

____

T F 4. The default theme font for headings is <u>Cambria</u>.

____

T F 5. A(n) <u>style</u> is a named group of formatting characteristics.

____

Definitions (5)

Briefly define each term.

1. insert mode ______________________________
2. drag-and-drop editing ______________________________
3. metadata ______________________________
4. point ______________________________
5. theme ______________________________

The Word Screen (5)

Identify the elements indicated in Figure WD1.

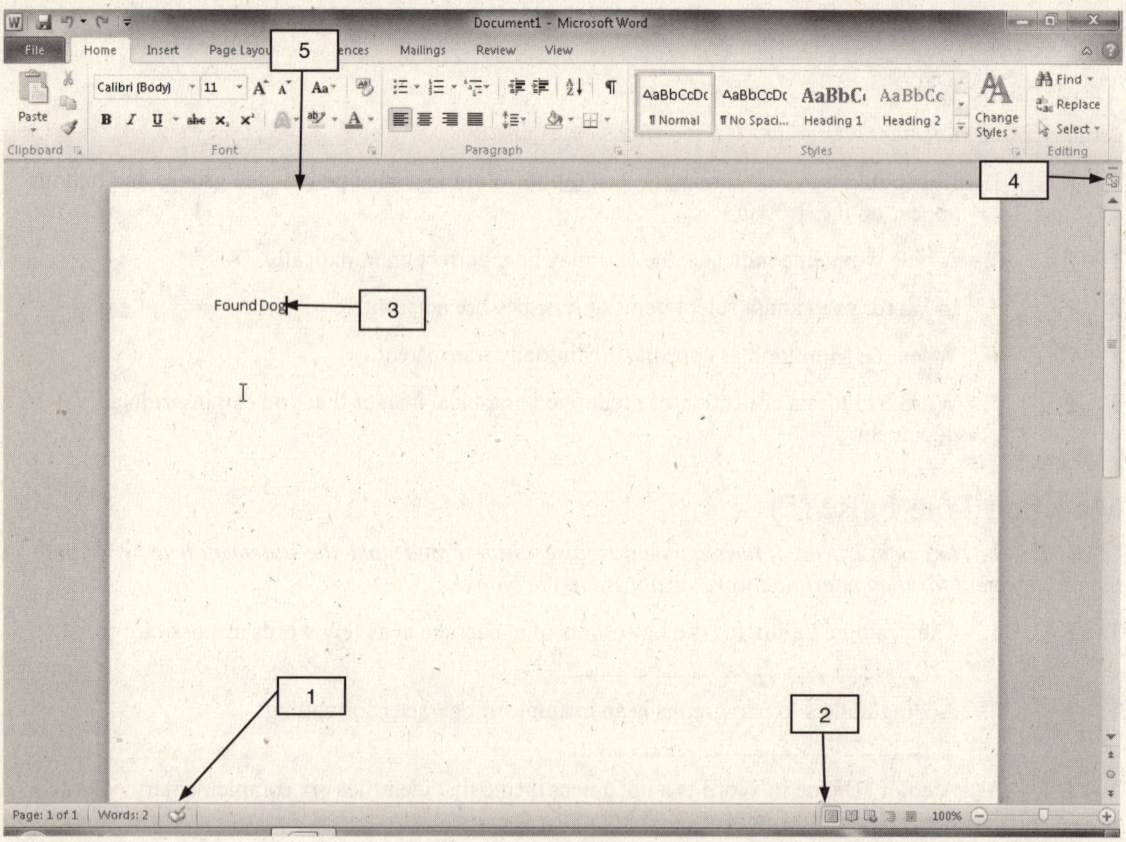

Figure WD1

1. ______________________________
2. ______________________________
3. ______________________________
4. ______________________________
5. ______________________________

Multiple Choice (5)

Circle the letter of the best answer.

1. Under which of the following circumstances should you not press the ENTER key?
   a. to insert a blank line in a document
   b. to begin a new paragraph
   c. to respond to a question in a Word dialog box
   d. when the insertion point reaches the right margin
2. How high is a character with a font size of 10 points?
   a. 10/12 of an inch
   b. 10/24 of an inch
   c. 10/36 of an inch
   d. 10/72 of an inch
3. What does a red wavy underline beneath a word mean?
   a. the word is misspelled
   b. the word is not in Word's dictionary
   c. the word contains a grammatical error
   d. Word can suggest a synonym
4. How can you scroll up one screen?
   a. click anywhere above the scroll box
   b. press CTRL+UP ARROW
   c. click the scroll arrow at the top of the scroll bar
   d. press CTRL+PAGE UP
5. What is the term for the small squares at each corner and the middle of the selection rectangle that surround a selected graphic?
   a. sizing handles
   b. reset buttons
   c. location squares
   d. formatting tabs

Dialog Box (5)

Answer the following questions about the Borders and Shading dialog box shown in Figure WD2.

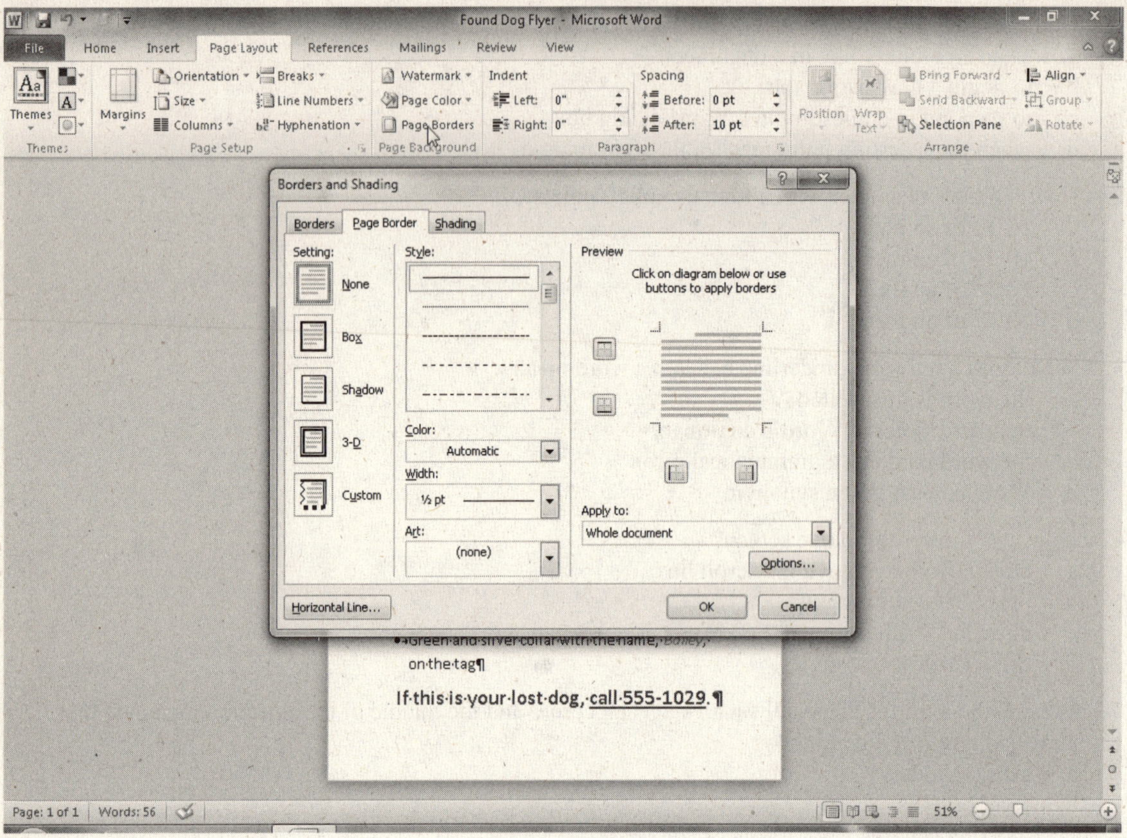

Figure WD2

1. How would you display this dialog box? ______________________________
2. How would you display the Color palette? ______________________________
3. What is the unit of measurement for the width of the page border? ______________________________
4. What is previewed on the right side of the dialog box? ______________________________
5. How do you remove a border shown in this dialog box? ______________________________

Fill in the Blanks (5)

Write a word (or words) in the blank to complete each sentence correctly.

1. ______________________ formatting is the process of changing the way characters appear on the screen and in print.
2. Each time you press the ______________________ key, Word creates a new paragraph.
3. When you ______________________ text, Word colors the rectangular area behind any text or graphics.
4. To change the font of characters in a headline, you first must ______________________, or highlight, the paragraphs in the headline.
5. ______________________ are words or phrases that further describe the document.

Sequence (5)

Use the numbers 1 – 5 to show the order in which these steps should be performed to open a document from Word.

___ Click Open in the Backstage view to display the Open dialog box.

___ Click File on the Ribbon to open the Backstage view.

___ Click the file to be opened.

___ Navigate to the location of the file to be opened.

___ Click the Open button to open the selected file and display the opened document in the Word window.

Complete the Table

SCROLLING WITH THE KEYBOARD

Scroll Direction	Key(s) to Press
Left one character	__________
__________	RIGHT ARROW
Left one word	__________
__________	CTRL+RIGHT ARROW
Up one line	__________
__________	DOWN ARROW
To end of line	__________
__________	HOME
Up one paragraph	__________
__________	CTRL+DOWN ARROW
Up one screen	__________
__________	PAGE DOWN
To top of document window	__________
__________	ALT+CTRL+PAGE DOWN
To beginning of document	__________
__________	CTRL+END

Short Answer (5)

Write a brief answer to each question.

1. What kind of errors can Word detect as you type?

2. Why are formatting marks recommended? How do you remove them if you do not want them to show on the screen?

3. What are some formatting suggestions to consider as you seek to improve the appearance of a flyer, for example?

4. What are some sources from which you can acquire graphical images?

5. What are some effects you apply to customize a picture?

Activities

Expanding on the Case

Perform the following tasks.

1. Open the Village Fireworks Flyer created in Cases and Places 3.
2. Change the font of the headline to 48-point Arial Rounded MT Bold, or a similar font.
3. Change the font size of the body copy to 22 point.
4. Change the sale price of the pork chop dinner to $5.00 in the body copy.
5. Change the sizes of the photographs in the flyer.
6. Add a border around the perimeter of the page. If there is an existing border, change its style.
7. Introduce a spelling mistake into the flyer to see the Spelling and Grammar Check in action.
8. Print the revised announcement.
9. Save the revised announcement as Village Fireworks Flyer_WKBK.

Expanding on the Lab

Perform the following tasks.

1. Open the Study Habits Flyer created in In the Lab 1.
2. Change the font of the headline to 48-point French Script MT, or a similar font.
3. Change expert to experienced in the first paragraph of the body copy.
4. Delete .00 in the first bullet of the body copy.
5. Change four weeks to four to six weeks in the second bullet of the body copy.
6. Change Let us help you! from bold to italic. Change the word *or* in the signature from italic to underlined.
7. Change the color of $15 to Dark Red, Accent 4.
8. Print the revised announcement.
9. Save the revised announcement as Lab 1-1 Study Habits Flyer_WKBK.

Microsoft Word 2010

Chapter Two
Creating a Research Paper with Citations and References

Overview

This chapter introduces you to changing document settings, using headers to number pages, modifying a style, inserting and editing citations and their sources, adding footnotes, creating a bibliographic list of sources, and using the Research task pane.

Chapter Outline

I. Introduction [WD 66]

A research paper is ____

II. Project — Research Paper [WD 66]

The Modern Language Association of America (MLA) and American Psychological Association (APA) are ____

A. Overview [WD 68]

To plagiarize means ____

B. MLA documentation style [WD 69]

Guidelines presented by the MLA:

- On all pages, double-space ____
  ____
  ____
  ____
- The title is ____
  ____
- Parenthetical references are ____
  ____
- Superscripts (raised numbers) signal ____
  ____
- The term works cited refers to ____
  ____

III. Changing document settings [WD 69]

The MLA documentation style defines some global formats that apply to the entire research paper.

A. Styles [WD 70]

A style is ______________________________

The Normal style is ______________________________

☞ To modify a style

1. ______________________________
2. ______________________________
3. ______________________________
____
4. ______________________________

B. Adjusting line and paragraph spacing [WD 72]

- Line spacing is ______________________________
- Paragraph spacing is ______________________________

Word, by default, single-spaces between lines of text. The MLA style requires that you double-space; that is, ______________________________

☞ To change line spacing

1. ______________________________
2. ______________________________

☞ To remove space after a paragraph

1. ______________________________
2. ______________________________

☞ To update a style to match a selection

1. ______________________________
2. ______________________________

C. Headers and footers [WD 75]

A header is ______________________________

A footer is ______________________________

☞ To switch to the header

1. ______________________________
____
2. ______________________________

☞ To right-align a paragraph

Right-aligned means ______________________________

1. ______________________________
____

☞ To insert a page number

1. ____________________

____

____

2. ____________________

☞ To close the header

1. ____________________

____

IV. Typing the research paper text [WD 78]

You can use Click and Type to ____________________

____

☞ To Click and Type

1. ____________________

____

2. ____________________

____

A. Shortcut keys [WD 81]

Shortcut keys (or keyboard key combinations) sometimes can be an efficient way to format text as you type.

☞ To format text using shortcut keys

1. ____________________

☞ To display the rulers

The horizontal ruler displays ____________________

The vertical ruler displays ____________________

1. ____________________

2. ____________________

First-line indent is a procedure in which the first line of each paragraph is ____________________

____

The First Line Indent marker is ____________________

The Left Indent marker is ____________________

☞ To first-line indent paragraphs

1. ____________________

2. ____________________

3. ____________________

4. ____________________

AutoCorrect automatically corrects ______________________________

____

☞ To AutoCorrect as you type

1. ______________________________

____

2. ______________________________

____

When you point near automatically corrected text, Word displays a small blue box. If you click the small blue box, Word displays the AutoCorrect Options button. If you click the AutoCorrect Options button, a menu is displayed that allows you to ______________________________

____

☞ To use the AutoCorrect Options button

1. ______________________________
2. ______________________________

____

____

You can add your own words to Word's predefined list of AutoCorrect entries.

☞ To create an AutoCorrect entry

1. ______________________________
2. ______________________________

____

____

3. ______________________________

____

B. The AutoCorrect dialog box [WD 87]

In addition to creating AutoCorrect entries for words you commonly misspell or mistype, you can create entries for abbreviations, codes, and so on.

C. Citations [WD 88]

The process for adding citations in Word is as follows:

1. ______________________________
2. ______________________________
3. ______________________________

☞ To change the bibliographic style

1. ______________________________

____

2. ______________________________

☞ To insert a citation and create its source

1. ______________________________

2. ______________________________

A field is ______________________________

3. ______________________________

____

____

4. ______________________________

____

☞ To edit a citation

1. ______________________________

____

2. ______________________________

____

3. ______________________________

4. ______________________________

____

D. Footnotes [WD 93]

A note reference mark signals ______________________________

____

A footnote is ______________________________

An endnote is ______________________________

Note text can be ______________________________

☞ To insert a footnote reference mark

1. ______________________________

____

____

☞ To insert a citation placeholder

1. ______________________________

2. ______________________________

____

A tag name is ______________________________

3. ______________________________

____

E. Footnote text style [WD 95]

☞ To modify a style using a shortcut menu

1. ______

2. ______

______

______

3. ______

______

4. ______

______

☞ To edit a source

1. ______

______

2. ______

______

______

3. ______

F. Working with footnotes and endnotes [WD 100]

The Word Count dialog box shows the number of words, pages, characters, paragraphs, and lines in a document.

☞ To count words

1. ______

______

2. ______

G. Automatic page breaks [WD 101]

Automatic, or soft, page breaks are ______

______

Background repagination is ______

V. Creating an alphabetical works cited page [WD 105]

The works cited page is ______

______

A bibliography is ______

A manual, or hard, page break is ______

______

☞ To page break manually

1. ______________________________

____

☞ To apply a style

1. ______________________________

____

☞ To create the bibliographical list

A bibliographical list is ______________________________

1. ______________________________

____

2. ______________________________

____

A hanging indent is ______________________________

The Hanging Indent marker is ______________________________

☞ To modify a source and update the bibliographical list

1. ______________________________

____

____

2. ______________________________

____

____

☞ To convert a field to regular text

1. ______________________________

2. ______________________________

VI. Proofing and revising the research paper [WD 112]

While proofreading, you look for ______________________________

____

☞ To scroll page by page through a document

1. ______________________________

____

A. Copying, cutting, and pasting [WD 113]

The Office Clipboard is ______________________________

____

Copying is ______________________________

Cutting is ______________________________

Pasting is ______________________________

☞ To copy and paste

1. ______________________________

____

2. ______________________________

3. ______________________________

☞ To display the Paste Options menu

1. ______________________________

2. ______________________________

☞ To find text

1. ______________________________

The Navigation Pane is ______________________________

2. ______________________________

3. ______________________________

☞ To replace text

1. ______________________________

____

2. ______________________________

3. ______________________________

B. Find and Replace dialog box [WD 117]

☞ To go to a page

1. ______________________________

2. ______________________________

3. ______________________________

☞ To find and insert a synonym

A synonym is ______________________________

A thesaurus is ______________________________

1. ______________________________

____

2. ______________________________

An antonym is______________________________

☞ To check spelling and grammar at once

1. ______________________________

____

2. ______________________________

____

3. ______________________________

____

4. ______________________________

____

C. The main and custom dictionaries [WD 120]

☞ To view or modify entries in a custom dictionary

1. ______________________________
2. ______________________________
3. ______________________________
4. ______________________________
5. ______________________________
6. ______________________________
7. ______________________________

☞ To set the default custom dictionary

1. ______________________________
2. ______________________________
3. ______________________________
4. ______________________________
5. ______________________________
6. ______________________________

☞ To use the Research task pane to look up information

1. ______________________________

____

2. ______________________________

____

3. ______________________________

D. Research task pane options [WD 122]

Clicking the Research Options link at the bottom of the Research task pane displays the _____

____

☞ To print document properties

1. ______________________________

____

____

2. ______________________________

____

____

☞ To preview the document and then print it

1. ____________________

   ____

   ____

   ____

2. ____________________
3. ____________________

   ____

4. ____________________

☞ To quit Word

1. ____________________
2. ____________________

Review

Matching (5)

Match each formatting task on the left with the appropriate shortcut keys from the right.

___ 1. all capital letters
___ 2. increase font size
___ 3. small capital letters
___ 4. decrease paragraph indent
___ 5. remove hanging indent

a. CTRL+SHIFT+K
b. CTRL+SHIFT+<
c. CTRL+SHIFT+T
d. CTRL+SHIFT+A
e. CTRL+SHIFT+M
f. CTRL+SHIFT+>
g. CTRL+SHIFT+W

True-False (5)

*Circle **T** if the statement is true and **F** if the statement is false.*

T F 1. The MLA style requires a title page.

T F 2. If used, explanatory notes elaborate on points discussed in the body of the paper.

T F 3. The Find and Replace Pane is a window that enables you to search for text in a document, browse through pages in a document, or browse through headings in a document.

T F 4. Word moves or adjusts manual page breaks; however, Word never adjusts any automatic page breaks that follow a manual page break.

T F 5. You can use drag-and-drop editing to move any selected item.

Modified True-False (5)

*Circle **T** if the statement is true. If the statement is false, circle **F** and make the statement true by writing the replacement for the underlined word or phrase in the blank.*

T F 1. When you install Word, it selects a series of services (reference books and Web sites) through which it searches when you use the Reference task pane.

____

T F 2. A(n) thesaurus is a book of synonyms.

____

T F 3. Clipping involves removing the selected item from the document and placing it on the Clipboard.

____

T F 4. Each time you press the SHIFT key, paragraph formatting in the previous paragraph carries forward to the next paragraph.

____

T F 5. A(n) bibliography is an alphabetical list of sources referenced in a paper.

____

Definitions (5)

Briefly define each term.

1. line spacing ____________________
2. first-line indent ____________________
3. works cited page ____________________
4. background repagination ____________________
5. anging indent ____________________

The Word Screen (5)

Identify the window elements indicated in Figure WD3.

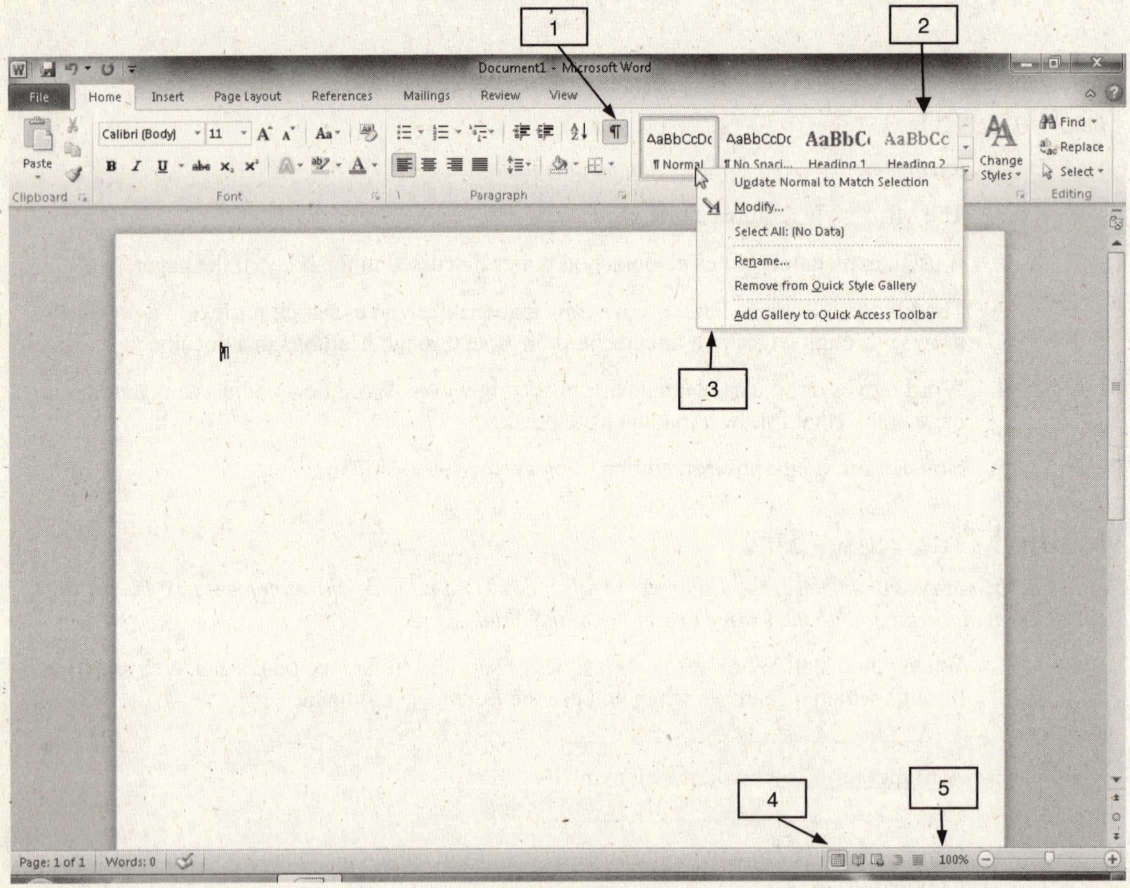

Figure WD3

1. ____________________
2. ____________________
3. ____________________
4. ____________________
5. ____________________

Multiple Choice (5)

Circle the letter of the best answer.

1. Which is *not* an MLA documentation style requirement?
   a. double-spaced text
   b. separate title page
   c. works cited page
   d. page numbers

2. What is the term for the text and graphics printed at the bottom of every page?
   a. tab
   b. leader
   c. header
   d. footer

3. Which keys do you press to center a paragraph before typing?
   a. CTRL+E
   b. CTRL+C
   c. CTRL+L
   d. CTRL+O

4. How would you first-line indent the paragraphs in a research paper one-half inch?
   a. drag the top triangle at the 0 mark on the ruler to the .5-inch mark
   b. drag the bottom triangle at the 0 mark on the ruler to the .5-inch mark
   c. drag the triangle at the 6.5-inch mark on the ruler to the 6-inch mark
   d. drag the small square at the 0 mark on the ruler to the .5-inch mark

5. Which of the following is *not* a type of information required by a Web site citation?
   a. publication year
   b. full name of author(s)
   c. title of Web site
   d. date viewed

Gallery (5)

Answer the following questions about the Header gallery shown in Figure WD4.

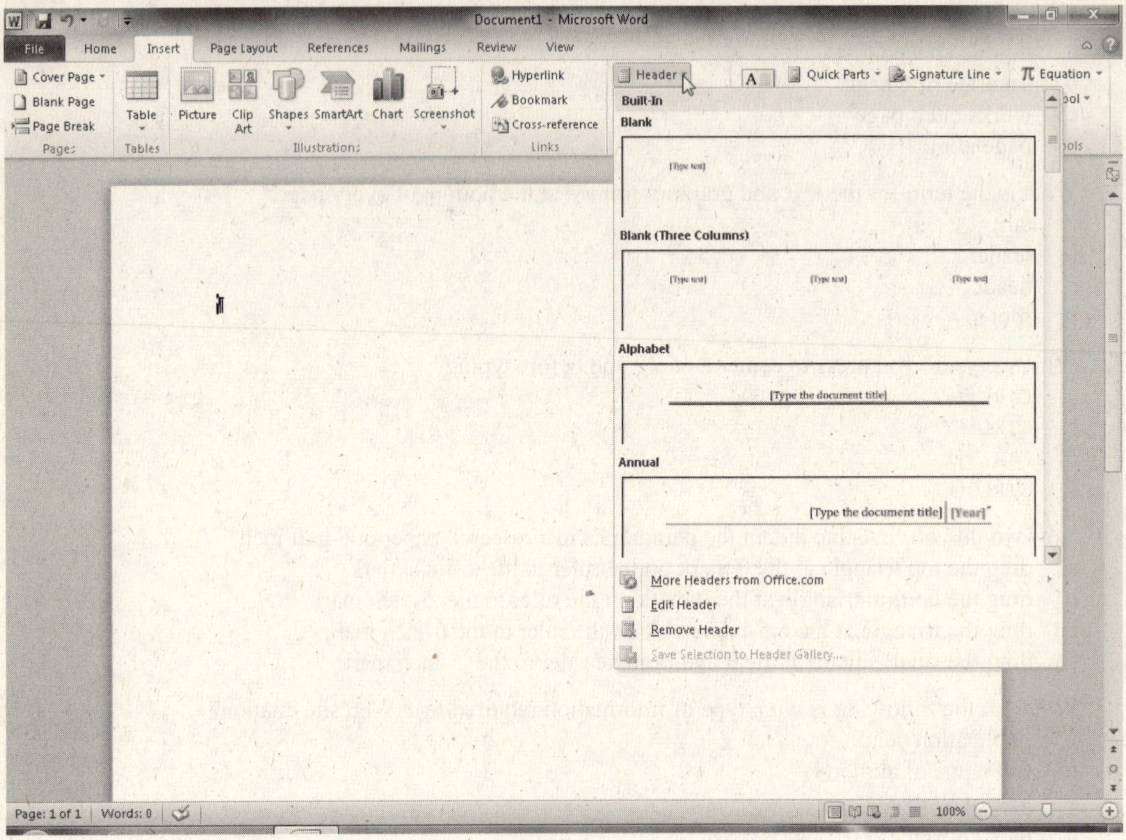

Figure WD4

1. How would you display this gallery? ______________________________
2. Which of the headers accessible from this gallery adheres to MLA documentation style? __________
3. How do you remove a header from a document? ______________________________
4. Which command in this gallery allows you to define your own header contents? ______________
5. Which command in this gallery deletes header contents from the entire document? ______________

Fill in the Blanks (5)

Write a word (or words) in the blank to complete each sentence correctly.

1. The MLA style uses in-text ____________________ instead of footnoting each source at the bottom of the page.
2. ____________________ is the process of copying an item from the Office Clipboard into the document at the location of the insertion point.
3. By default, the Normal style places 10 points of blank space after each ____________________.

4. When you use ________________________, you double-click a blank area of the document window, and Word automatically formats the item you enter according to the location where you double-click.

5. Word can format a list of sources and alphabetize them in a(n) ________________________, saving you time looking up style guidelines.

Sequence (5)

Use the numbers 1 – 5 to show the order in which these steps should be performed to set the default custom dictionary.

____ Click the Change Default button in the Custom Dictionaries dialog box.

____ Click Proofing in the left pane of the Word Options dialog box, and then click the Custom Dictionaries button.

____ In the Custom Dictionaries dialog box, place a check mark next to the desired dictionary name.

____ Click File on the Ribbon and then click Options in the Backstage view.

____ Click the OK button in the Custom Dictionaries dialog box; if the Suggest from main dictionary only check box is selected in the Word Options dialog box, remove the check mark and click the OK button.

Complete the Table

SHORTCUT KEYS FOR FORMATTING CHARACTERS

Character Formatting Task	Shortcut Keys
________________________	CTRL+SHIFT+A
Bold	________________________
________________________	SHIFT+F3
Decrease font size	________________________
Decrease font size 1 point	________________________
Double-underline	________________________
Italic	________________________
Remove character formatting (plain text)	________________________
Small uppercase letters	________________________
Subscript	________________________
Underline	________________________

Short Answer (5)

Write a brief answer to each question.

1. Why would you use a keyboard shortcut, instead of the Ribbon, to format text?

2. What is the difference between a soft page break and a hard page break?

3. What is a tag name?

4. What is the purpose of the commands on the Paste Options menu?

5. What should you do if the synonyms list on the shortcut menu does not display a suitable word?

Activities

Expanding on Apply Your Knowledge

Perform the following tasks.

1. Open the file named Apply 2-1 Space Paragraph Draft that you created in Apply Your Knowledge.
2. Select the paragraph of text in the document and change its line spacing from double to 1.5.
3. Use the thesaurus to replace the word, important, in the first sentence of the first paragraph with an appropriate synonym.
4. Add a footnote at the end of the paragraph, to read as follows: More information about the detectors used by NASA can be found on the following Web site: http://ranier.hq.nasa.gov/sensors_page/insthp.html.
5. Use the Find dialog box to replace all occurrences of the word, sensors, with the word, detectors.
6. Print the revised paper.
7. Save the revised paper as Apply 2-1 Space Paragraph Draft_WKBK.

Expanding on the Lab

Perform the following tasks.

1. Open the file named Lab 2-1 Short Research Paper that you created in In the Lab 1.
2. Add a footnote to the last sentence of the third paragraph of the report, to read as follows: More information about Bluetooth technology is available at www.bluetooth.com.
3. Use the thesaurus to replace the word, elements, in the first sentence of the third paragraph with an appropriate synonym.
4. Add an entry to the end of the works cited page, as follows: Carr, Diane et al. *Computer Games: Text, Narrative and Play*. Boston: Polity, 2006. Print.
5. Sort the works cited in ascending order.
6. Print the revised paper.
7. Save the revised paper as Lab 2-1 Short Research Paper_WKBK.

Microsoft Word 2010

Chapter Three
Creating a Business Letter with a Letterhead and Table

Overview

This chapter introduces how to use Word to change margins, insert and format a shape, change text wrapping, insert and format clip art, move and copy graphics, insert symbols, add a border, clear formatting, convert a hyperlink to regular text, create a file from an existing file, set and use tab stops, insert the current date, create and insert building blocks, insert and format tables, and address and print envelopes and mailing labels.

Chapter Outline

I. Introduction [WD 138]

In a business environment, people use documents to communicate with others.

II. Project — Business Letter with a Letterhead [WD 138]

A. Overview [WD 140]

A letterhead is ____

____

☞ To change margin settings

1. ____

____

2. ____

III. Creating a letterhead [WD 142]

☞ To insert a shape

A drawing object is ____

1. ____

2. ____

____

3. ____

4. ____

____

☞ To apply a shape style

1. ______________________________

____

2. ______________________________

☞ To add text to a shape

1. ______________________________

2. ______________________________

____

☞ To use the Grow Font button to increase font size

1. ______________________________

2. ______________________________

____

A. Floating versus inline objects [WD 147]

An inline object is ______________________________

A floating object is ______________________________

☞ To change an object's text wrapping

1. ______________________________

____

2. ______________________________

____

☞ To insert clip art

Clip art is ______________________________

The Clip Organizer contains ______________________________

____

1. ______________________________

____

____

2. ______________________________

____

3. ______________________________

☞ To resize a graphic to a percent of the original

1. ______________________________

____

2. ______________________________

____

3. ______________________________

☞ To change the color of a graphic

1. ______________________________

____

2. ______________________________

☞ To set a transparent color in a graphic

When you make one color in a graphic transparent, you ______________________________

____

1. ______________________________

2. ______________________________

____

3. ______________________________

____

☞ To adjust the brightness and contrast of a graphic

1. ______________________________

2. ______________________________

☞ To change the border color on a graphic

1. ______________________________

____

2. ______________________________

☞ To move a graphic

1. ______________________________

2. ______________________________

☞ To use paste options

1. ______________________________

____

2. ______________________________

☞ To flip a graphic

1. ______________________________

____

2. ______________________________

☞ To insert a symbol from the Symbol dialog box

1. ______________________________

____

2. ______________________________

____

____

3. ____________________

☞ To insert a symbol from the Symbol gallery

1. ____________________

2. ____________________

3. ____________________

☞ To bottom border a paragraph

A border is ____________________

1. ____________________

____

2. ____________________

☞ To clear formatting

The term clear formatting refers to ____________________

____

1. ____________________

____

2. ____________________

____

B. AutoFormat As You Type [WD 162]

As you type text in a document, Word automatically formats some of it for you.

☞ To convert a hyperlink to regular text

1. ____________________

2. ____________________

____

IV. Creating a business letter [WD 164]

☞ To create a new file from an existing file

1. ____________________

____

2. ____________________

____

3. ____________________

☞ To apply a Quick Style

1. ____________________

____

Essential elements of a letter include the following:

The date line, which consists of ____________________

The inside address, which usually contains ______________________

____

The salutation, which begins ______________________

The message, which begins ______________________

The complimentary close, which displays ______________________

The signature block, which displays ______________________

A. Using tab stops to align text [WD 168]

A tab stop is ______________________

____

☞ To set custom tab stops

1. ______________________

____

____

2. ______________________

When you press the TAB key, ______________________

____

☞ To insert the current date in a document

1. ______________________

____

____

2. ______________________

☞ To create a building block

A building block contains ______________________

____

1. ______________________

____

2. ______________________

____

3. ______________________

____

☞ To modify a building block

1. ______________________

____

2. ______________________

____

3. ______________________

☞ To insert a building block

1. ____________________

____

2. ____________________

B. Building blocks versus AutoCorrect [WD 174]

The difference between an AutoCorrect entry and a building block entry is ____________________

____

☞ To insert a nonbreaking space

A nonbreaking space is ____________________

____

A nonbreaking hyphen is ____________________

____

1. ____________________

____

____

2. ____________________

____

C. Tables [WD 176]

A Word table is ____________________

A cell is ____________________

The dimension of a table is ____________________

☞ To insert an empty table

1. ____________________

____

2. ____________________

3. ____________________

An end-of-cell mark is ____________________

An end-of-row mark can be used to ____________________

☞ To enter data in a table

To advance rightward from one cell to the next, ____________________

When you are at the rightmost cell in a row, to move to the first cell in the next row, you should press ____________________

One way to add new rows to a table is to ____________________

____

1. ______________________________________

____

____

☞ To apply a table style

1. ______________________________________

____

2. ______________________________________

____

3. ______________________________________

____

☞ To resize table columns to fit table contents

1. ______________________________________

____

2. ______________________________________

____

A column boundary is ______________________________________

A row boundary is ______________________________________

The table resize handle is ______________________________________

D. Selecting table contents [WD 181]

Word offers a variety of ways to select items in a table.

☞ To align data in cells

1. ______________________________________

2. ______________________________________

☞ To center a table

1. ______________________________________

2. ______________________________________

3. ______________________________________

☞ To insert a row in a table

1. ______________________________________

2. ______________________________________

☞ To insert a column in a table

1. ______________________________________

2. ______________________________________

____

E. Deleting table data [WD 185]

To delete rows or columns from a table ______________________________

____

To delete the contents of a cell ______________________________

☞ To merge cells

1. ______________________________
2. ______________________________

☞ To split table cells

1. ______________________________
2. ______________________________
3. ______________________________
4. ______________________________

☞ To bullet a list as you type

1. ______________________________
2. ______________________________

____

3. ______________________________

____

V. Addressing and printing envelopes and mailing labels [WD 189]

With Word, you can print address information on an envelope or on a mailing label.

☞ To address and print an envelope

1. ______________________________

____

2. ______________________________

____

____

3. ______________________________

____

A. Envelopes and labels [WD 189]

To specify a different envelope or label type, click the ______________________________

____

Review

Matching (5)

Match each term on the left with the best description from the right.

___ 1. table
___ 2. cell
___ 3. end-of-cell mark
___ 4. column boundary
___ 5. table resize handle

a. item dragged to change a table to a new size
b. intersection of a row and a column
c. collection of rows and columns
d. similar to a form with prewritten text
e. formatting mark used to select and format cells
f. border to the right of a column
g. temporary Windows storage area

True-False (5)

*Circle **T** if the statement is true and **F** if the statement is false.*

T F 1. The total number of rows and columns required by a table is called its resolution.

T F 2. Essential business letter elements include the date line, inside address, message, and signature block.

T F 3. When you set a custom tab stop, Word clears all default tab stops to the right of the custom tab stop.

T F 4. In the block style, all components of the letter begin flush with the left margin.

T F 5. When you are in the rightmost cell in a row, press the ENTER key to move to the first cell in the next row of the table.

Modified True-False (5)

*Circle **T** if the statement is true. If the statement is <u>false</u>, circle **F** and make the statement true by writing the replacement for the underlined word or phrase in the blank.*

T F 1. You can make one color in a graphic <u>opaque</u>; that is, remove the color.

____

T F 2. If you use the same text frequently, you can store the text in a(n) <u>content control</u> and then use that stored entry in the open (or future) documents.

____

T F 3. The term <u>clear</u> formatting refers to returning the formatting to the Normal style.

____

T F 4. A predefined graphic is called <u>clip art</u>.

____

T F 5. A(n) <u>floating</u> object is an object that is part of a paragraph.

____

Definitions (5)

Briefly define each term.

1. floating object ______________________________
2. border ______________________________
3. building block ______________________________
4. tab character ______________________________
5. nonbreaking space ______________________________

The Word Screen (5)

Identify the elements of the Word window in Figure WD5.

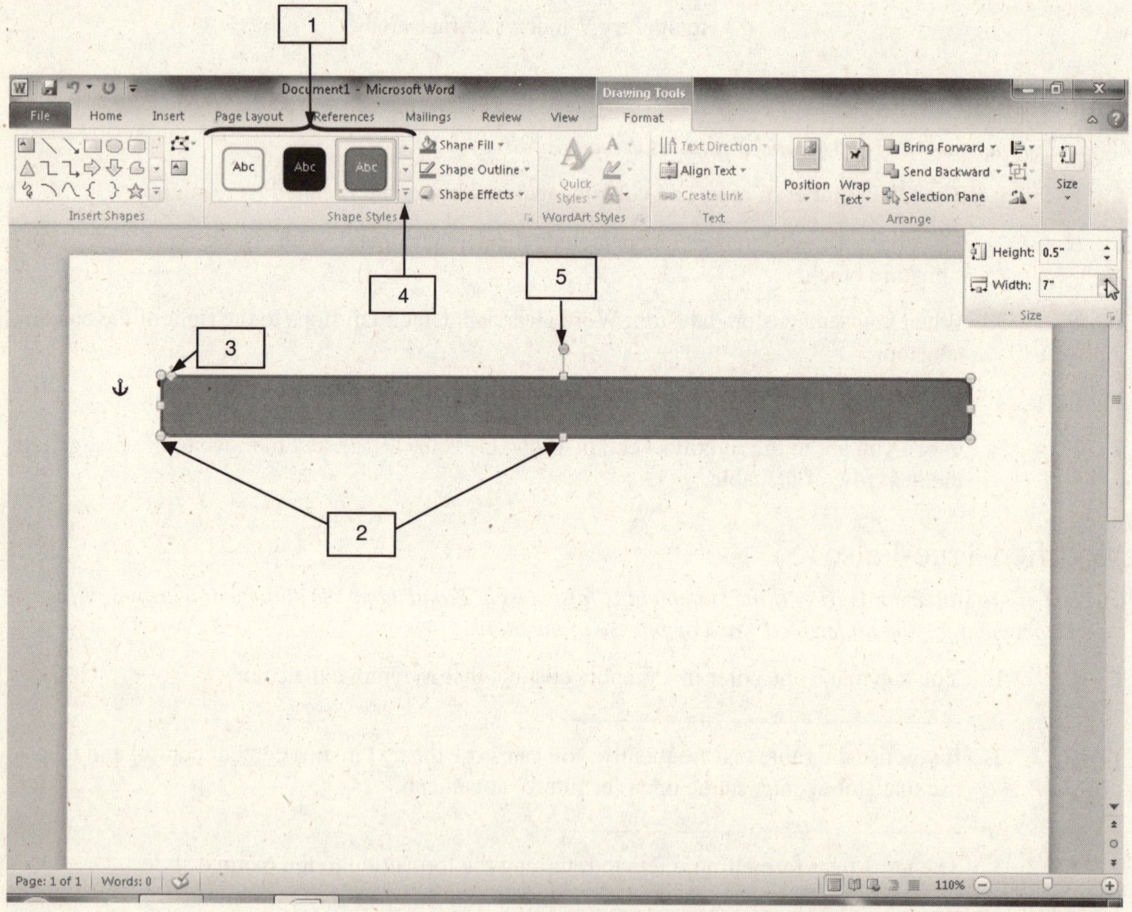

Figure WD5

1. ______________________________
2. ______________________________
3. ______________________________
4. ______________________________
5. ______________________________

Multiple Choice (5)

Circle the letter of the best answer.

1. Given the AutoFormat As You Type options, what happens when you type text, a space, one hyphen, one or no spaces, text, and then a space?
   a. the AutoFormat feature changes the hyphen to an em dash
   b. the AutoFormat feature changes the hyphen to an en dash
   c. the AutoFormat feature makes part of the ordinal a superscript
   d. the AutoFormat feature places a border above the paragraph

2. Which of the following is a text wrapping option that works with inline objects?
   a. Top and Bottom
   b. Tight
   c. Through
   d. In Line with Text

3. What is the term for a predefined style you can use in Word to format text?
   a. style control
   b. style block
   c. AutoStyle
   d. Quick Style

4. What do you press to enter a special type of hyphen that prevents two words separated by a hyphen from splitting at the end of a line?
   a. CTRL+SHIFT+HYPHEN
   b. ALT+CTRL+HYPHEN
   c. SHIFT+ALT+HYPHEN
   d. TAB+ALT+HYPHEN

5. By default, where does Word place tab stops on the ruler?
   a. at every .125-inch mark
   b. at every .25-inch mark
   c. at every .5-inch mark
   d. at every 1-inch mark

Gallery (5)

Answer the following questions about the Table gallery shown in Figure WD6.

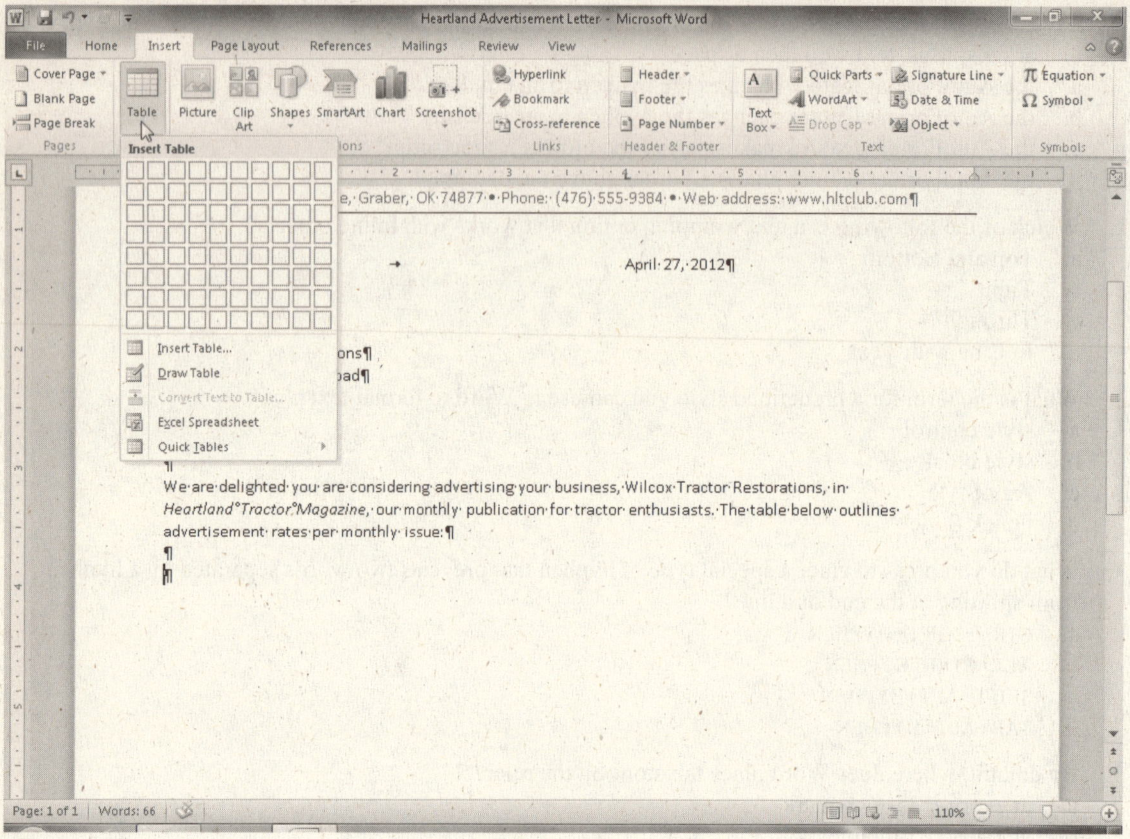

Figure WD6

1. How do you select the desired table dimension using the gallery shown? ______________________
____

2. Where will an inserted table display in the document? ______________________

3. In a table inserted using this gallery, what formatting mark will assist you with selecting and formatting cells? ______________________

4. In a table inserted using this gallery, what mark can you use to add columns to the right of a table?
____

5. How do you display a preview of the desired table dimensions? ______________________
____

Fill in the Blanks (5)

Write a word (or words) in the blank to complete each sentence correctly.

1. To change the width of a column, hold down the ______________________ key while dragging markers on the ruler.

2. Default tab marks are indicated on the horizontal ruler by small vertical ______________________.

3. In Word you can draw a solid line, called a(n) ______________________, at any edge of a paragraph.

4. In the _________________________ letter, the date, complimentary close, and signature block are positioned approximately .5 inch to the right of the center or at the right margin, and all other letter components begin flush with the left margin.

5. The _________________________ of a table is the total number of rows and columns.

Sequence (5)

Use the numbers 1 – 5 to show the order in which these steps should be performed to create a building block.

___ Type the desired name of the building block.

___ Select the text to be a building block, without selecting the paragraph mark at the end of the text.

___ Click Save Selection to Quick Part Gallery on the Quick Parts menu.

___ Click the OK button.

___ Click the Quick Parts button on the Insert tab.

Complete the Table

SELECTING ITEMS IN A TABLE

Item to Select	Action
Cell	____________________
Column	____________________
____________________ ____________________	Drag through cells, rows, or columns
____________________ ____________________	Select first cell, row, or column and then hold down CTRL key while selecting next cell, row, or column
____________________	Press TAB
____________________	Press SHIFT+TAB
Row	____________________ ____________________
Table	____________________ ____________________

Short Answer (5)

Write a brief answer to each question.

1. How do you remove an existing border from a paragraph?

2. What is the purpose of the tab selector?

3. When should the Update automatically check box in the Date and Time dialog box be checked?

4. What are the small circles in the cells of a table?

5. What is the difference between an AutoCorrect entry and a building block entry?

Activities

Expanding on Make It Right

Perform the following tasks.

1. Open the document created in Make It Right.
2. Replace the clip art image, and change the color of the text in the letterhead to match a color in the graphic.
3. Change the letter to the modified semi-block style.
4. Sort the table by the items in the second column of the table.
5. Left-align the table.
6. Italicize the contents of the second column of the table.
7. Apply a different table style of your choice to the table.
8. Print the revised announcement.
9. Save the revised announcement with a suffix of _WKBK.doc.

Expanding on the Lab

Perform the following tasks.

1. Open the file named Lab 3-2 Library Letter that you created in In the Lab 2.
2. Change the theme fonts to Monotype Corsiva.
3. Change the color of the e-mail address, mtlawrence@jpl.net, to dark red.
4. Use drag-and-drop editing techniques to switch, Blank CD or DVD to store documents and notes created during class, with, Your valid library card to verify enrollment eligibility, in the bulleted list.
5. Add a row to the table for an additional course, with details of your choosing.
6. Change Room 10B to Room 12A in both places where it appears in the table.
7. Italicize Head Librarian in the signature.
8. View the revised letter from within print preview. If the letter exceeds one page, use the Shrink to Fit button on the Print Preview toolbar to shrink it to a page. Print the revised resume.
9. Save the revised resume as Lab 3-2 Library Letter_WKBK.

Microsoft PowerPoint 2010

Chapter One
Creating and Editing a Presentation with Clip Art

Overview

In this chapter, you learn how to apply a document theme; create a title slide and text slides with a bulleted list, clip art, and a photograph; size and move clip art and a photograph; format and edit text; add a slide transition; view the presentation in Slide Show view; and print slides as handouts.

Chapter Outline

I. Introduction [PPT 2]

A presentation also is called a(n) ______________________________

II. Project — Presentation with Bulleted Lists and Clip Art [PPT 2]

A. Overview [PPT 4]

The general guidelines to follow when creating a presentation are

1. ______________________________

____

2. ______________________________

3. ______________________________

Format means ______________________________

4. ______________________________

To save a presentation means ______________________________

5. ______________________________

☞ To start PowerPoint

1. ______________________________

2. ______________________________

3. ______________________________

4. ______________________________

III. Choosing a document theme [PPT 5]

A document theme provides ______________________________

☞ To choose a document theme

Until you select a different theme, PowerPoint initially uses the ______________

1. ______________
2. ______________

____
3. ______________

☞ To enter the presentation subtitle paragraph

1. ______________
2. ______________

IV. Formatting characters in a presentation [PPT 10]

A. Fonts and font styles [PPT 10]

Format is ______________

Font (or typeface) defines ______________

Style indicates how ______________

Size specifies ______________

A point is ______________

Color defines ______________

☞ To select a paragraph

1. ______________

☞ To italicize text

1. ______________

☞ To increase font size

1. ______________

____

☞ To select a word

1. ______________
2. ______________

☞ To change the text color

1. ______________

____

2. ______________
3. ______________

V. Adding a new slide to a presentation [PPT 14]

☞ To add a new text slide with a bulleted list

1. ______________

2. ______________________________

____

VI. Creating a text slide with a single-level bulleted list [PPT 15]

A bulleted list is ______________________________

A multi-level bulleted list slide consists of ______________________________

☞ To enter a slide title

1. ______________________________

☞ To select a text placeholder

1. ______________________________

☞ To add a new slide and enter a slide title

1. ______________________________

2. ______________________________

☞ To type a multi-level bulleted list

Demoting text means ______________________________

Promoting text means ______________________________

1. ______________________________

2. ______________________________

____

3. ______________________________

4. ______________________________

☞ To select a group of words

1. ______________________________

2. ______________________________

☞ To bold text

1. ______________________________

VII. Adding new slides and changing slide layouts [PPT 21]

The Layout gallery is used to ______________________________

A custom layout specifies ______________________________

☞ To add a slide with the Title Only layout

1. ______________________________

____

2. ______________________________

☞ To add a new slide and enter a slide title and headings

1. ______________________________

2. ______________________________

____

____

3. ______________________________

A. PowerPoint views [PPT 24]

A view is ______________________________

Normal view is composed of ______________________________

The left side of the screen in Normal view has a Tabs pane that consists of ______________________________

____

The Slide pane shows ______________________________

The Notes pane is an area where you can ______________________________

Notes Page view displays ______________________________

You can drag the splitter bar to ______________________________

After you have created at least two slides, a scroll bar containing scroll arrows and scroll boxes will appear on the right edge of the window.

☞ To move to another slide in Normal view

The slide indicator shows ______________________________

1. ______________________________

____

2. ______________________________

3. ______________________________

VIII. Inserting clip art and photographs into slides [PPT 26]

A clip is ______________________________

Microsoft Clip Organizer contains ______________________________

The Office Collections contains ______________________________

My Collections stores ______________________________

Files in the Shared Collections typically reside ______________________________

____

The Web Collections clips reside ______________________________

____

A. The Clip Art task pane [PPT 26]

The Clip Art task pane allows you to ______________________________

____

Clip collections combine ______________________________

☞ To insert a clip from the Clip Organizer into the title slide

1. ______________________________

2. ______________________________

☞ To insert a clip from the Clip Organizer into a content placeholder

1. ______________________________

2. ______________________________

3. ______________________________

4. ______________________________

IX. Photographs and the Clip Organizer [PPT 31]

In addition to clip art, you can insert pictures into a presentation. Some of the formats recognized by PowerPoint include: ______________________________

X. Resizing clip art and photographs [PPT 33]

Resizing includes ______________________________

A selection rectangle is ______________________________

Sizing handles are ______________________________

☞ To resize clip art

1. ______________________________

2. ______________________________

3. ______________________________

☞ To move clips

1. ______________________________

____

____

2. ______________________________

____

____

3. ______________________________

____

4. ______________________________

____

XI. Ending a slide show with a closing slide [PPT 38]

☞ To duplicate a slide

1. ______________________________

2. ______________________________

☞ To arrange a slide

Drag and drop is ______________________________

1. ______________________________

XII. Making changes to slide text content [PPT 40]

You generally make three types of changes to text in a presentation:

Additions are necessary ______________________________

____

Replacements are needed ______________________________

____

Deletions are required ______________________________

____

A. Replacing text in an existing slide [PPT 41]

When you need to correct a word or phrase, you can replace the text by ______________

____

PowerPoint inserts text to the left of the insertion point. The text to the right of the insertion point moves to the right to accommodate the added text.

B. Deleting text [PPT 41]

☞ To delete text in a placeholder

1. ______________________________

____

2. ____________________

3. ____________________

4. ____________________

C. Adding a transition [PPT 43]

Animation includes ____________________

A slide transition is ____________________

☞ To add a transition between slides

1. ____________________

2. ____________________

____

3. ____________________

____

4. ____________________

5. ____________________

XIII. Changing document properties [PPT 45]

Document properties (metadata) are ____________________

A keyword is ____________________

Standard properties are ____________________

Automatically updated properties include ____________________

____

☞ To change document properties

The Document Information Panel contains ____________________

1. ____________________

____

2. ____________________

3. ____________________

4. ____________________

____

____

5. ____________________

XIV. Viewing the presentation in Slide Show view [PPT 47]

☞ To start Slide Show view

You use Slide Show view when ____________________

1. ____________________

____

2. ______________________________

☞ To move manually through slides in a slide show

1. ______________________________
2. ______________________________

☞ To quit PowerPoint

1. ______________________________
2. ______________________________

XV. Printing a presentation [PPT 51]

A hard copy, or printout, is ______________________________

Printed copies of your document can be useful for the following reasons:

- ______________________________
- ______________________________

Green computing involves ______________________________

☞ To print a presentation

1. ______________________________
   ____
2. ______________________________
3. ______________________________
   ____

Review

Matching (5)

Match each term on the left with the best description from the right.

___ 1. Clip Organizer
___ 2. Office Collections
___ 3. My Collections
___ 4. Shared Collections
___ 5. Web Collections

a. contains all the media files included with Microsoft Office
b. where media files that you create are stored
c. a collection of drawings, photographs, sounds, videos, and other media files shared among Microsoft Office applications
d. typically reside on a network file server
e. allows you to search for clips by using descriptive keywords
f. accessible only when editing a presentation in Normal view
g. available only if you have an active Internet connection

True-False (5)

*Circle **T** if the statement is true and **F** if the statement is false.*

T F 1. PowerPoint assumes every new slide has a title.

T F 2. To use a clip from Microsoft Clip Organizer, be certain you have the legal right to insert this file in your presentation.

T F 3. PowerPoint allows you to wrap text around a picture or other graphic.

T F 4. When you run a slide show, the PowerPoint window is hidden.

T F 5. When making a presentation, you use Normal view.

Modified True-False (5)

*Circle **T** if the statement is true. If the statement is false, circle **F** and make the statement true by writing the replacement for the underlined word or phrase in the blank.*

T F 1. The default slide layouts are set up in portrait orientation.

____

T F 2. A slide that consists of more than one level of bulleted text is called a multi-level bulleted list slide.

____

T F 3. Creating a higher-level paragraph is called elevating text.

____

T F 4. You can type the text of a presentation on the Outline tab and easily rearrange bulleted lists, paragraphs, and slides.

____

T F 5. A hard copy is information that exists on a physical medium such as paper.

____

Definitions (5)

Briefly define each term.

1. resizing ______________________________
2. size ______________________________
3. format ______________________________
4. paragraph ______________________________
5. level ______________________________

The PowerPoint Screen (5)

Identify the elements indicated in Figure PPT1.

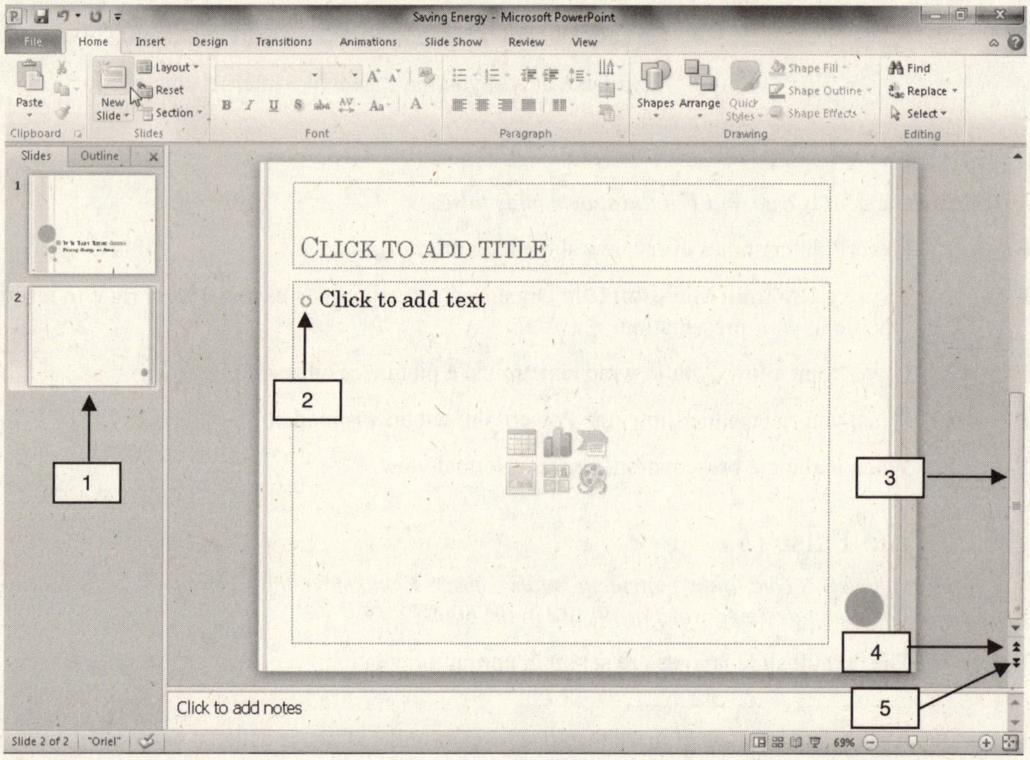

Figure PPT1

1. ______________________ 4. ______________________
2. ______________________ 5. ______________________
3. ______________________

Multiple Choice (5)

Circle the letter of the best answer.

1. On which of the following can you save a presentation?
   a. USB flash drive
   b. hard disk
   c. CD
   d. all of the above

2. What is the maximum distance that audience members generally will sit from a screen?
   a. 10 feet
   b. 30 feet
   c. 50 feet
   d. There is no agreed-upon maximum.

3. What kind of text has a slanted appearance?
   a. bold
   b. shaded
   c. italicized
   d. parsed

4. Which of the following is *not* one of PowerPoint's main views?
   a. Normal
   b. Slide Sorter
   c. Reading
   d. Notebook

5. What does PowerPoint do to an image when you add it to a presentation?
   a. rasterizes it
   b. compresses it
   c. concatenates it
   d. outlines it

Panel (5)

Answer the following questions about the Document Information Panel shown in Figure PPT2.

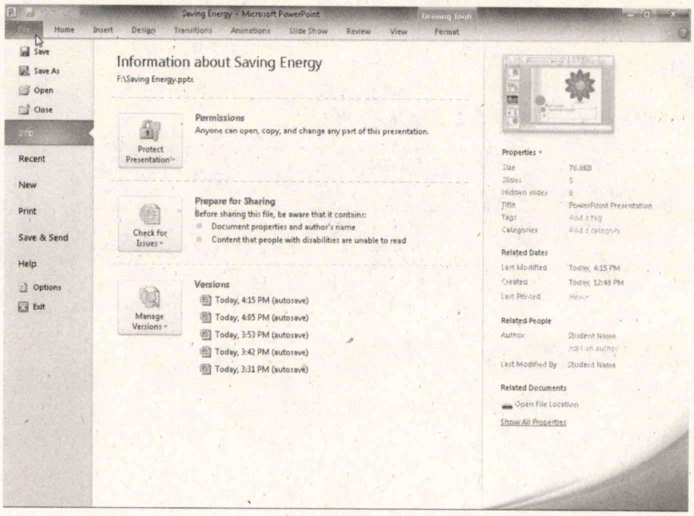

Figure PPT2

1. How was this panel displayed? ______________________________
2. What is previewed at the top of the right pane? ______________________________
3. What is automatically displayed in the right pane of this gallery? ______________________________
   ____
4. How do you close the Backstage view? ______________________________
5. When can you view and change information in this panel? ______________________________
   ____

Fill in the Blanks (5)

Write a word (or words) in the blank to complete each sentence correctly.

1. A PowerPoint presentation also is called a(n) ________________________.
2. A(n) ________________________ is a box with dotted or hatch-marked borders that are displayed when you create a new slide.
3. If no standard layout meets your design needs, you can create a(n) ________________________ layout.
4. A(n) ________________________ is a word or phrase that further describes a document.
5. ________________________ involves reducing the environmental waste generated when using a computer.

Sequence (5)

Use the numbers 1 – 5 to show the order in which these steps should be performed to add a transition between slides.

___ Click the More button to expand the Transitions gallery.

___ Click the desired duration.

___ Click the Transitions tab on the Ribbon.

___ Click the Apply to All button.

___ Click the desired transition.

Complete the Table

PRIMARY FILE FORMATS POWERPOINT RECOGNIZES

Format	File Extension
________________	.eps
________________	.gif
Windows Bitmap	________________________
Joint Photographic Experts Group (JPEG)	________________________
WordPerfect Graphics	________________________
Portable Network Graphics	________________________

Short Answer (5)

Write a brief answer to each question.

1. What is the 7 x 7 rule?

2. Of what is the Normal view composed?

3. What is the difference between a selection rectangle and sizing handles?

4. What is a black slide?

5. How can you ensure that your presentation will open in PowerPoint 2003 or older versions of this software?

Activities

Expanding on Make It Right

Perform the following tasks.

1. Open the Make It Right 1-1 Ducts presentation created in Make It Right.
2. Change the document theme from Module to Metro.
3. On Slide 2, change the title text font size to 36.
4. On Slide 3, change the title text font size to 36, and increase the size of clip.
5. Move Slide 3 to become the new Slide 2.
6. Introduce a spelling mistake into the presentation to see the Spelling and Grammar Check in action.
7. Print the revised presentation.
8. Save the revised presentation as Make It Right 1-1 Ducts_WKBK.

Expanding on the Lab

Perform the following tasks.

1. Open the Lab 1-1 Study Skills presentation created in In the Lab 1.
2. Change the title of Slide 1 to Be Prepared and italicize the subtitle. Make the same changes to Slide 4.
3. On Slide 2, change the last second level bulleted paragraph to Summarize key points.
4. On Slide 3, delete the bulleted paragraph, Wear comfy clothes.
5. On Slide 3, add At least 10 minutes before the start as a third-level paragraph under the Be early bullet.
6. Check the spelling of your presentation.
7. Display the revised presentation in black and white.
8. Print the revised black and white presentation.
9. Save the revised presentation as Lab 1-1 Study Skills_WKBK.

Microsoft PowerPoint 2010

Chapter Two
Enhancing a Presentation with Pictures, Shapes, and WordArt

Overview

In this chapter, you learn how to add a background style, insert and format pictures, add shapes, size graphic elements, apply styles, and insert WordArt.

Chapter Outline

I. Introduction [PPT 74]

Whether reading a document or viewing a PowerPoint presentation, people increasingly want to see photographs, artwork, graphics, and a variety of typefaces.

II. Project — Presentation with Pictures, Shapes, and WordArt [PPT 74]

A. Overview [PPT 74]

The following are general guidelines for creating a presentation with illustrations:

1. ______________________________

2. ______________________________

____

3. ______________________________

____

4. ______________________________

____

5. ______________________________

____

6. ______________________________

____

III. Starting PowerPoint [PPT 76]

IV. Creating slides and changing font colors and background style [PPT 77]

A. Presentation template color scheme [PPT 80]

The color scheme consists of ______________________________

____

The components of a color scheme include:

- ______
- ______
- ______
- ______

☞ To change the presentation theme colors

1. ______

2. ______

B. Inserting and formatting pictures in a presentation [PPT 82]

☞ To insert a picture

1. ______

2. ______

3. ______

A selection rectangle is ______

Sizing handles display at ______

☞ To insert a picture into a slide without a content placeholder

1. ______

2. ______

3. ______

☞ To correct a picture

Brightness determines ______

Contrast is ______

1. ______

☞ To apply a picture style

A style is ______________________________

1. ______________________________

____

____

2. ______________________________

☞ To apply picture effects

1. ______________________________

____

____

2. ______________________________

3. ______________________________

____

____

4. ______________________________

☞ To apply a picture border

1. ______________________________

2. ______________________________

____

____

3. ______________________________

☞ To change a picture border color

1. ______________________________

2. ______________________________

____

____

3. ______________________________

☞ To resize a graphic by entering exact measurements

1. ______________________________

____

2. ______________________________

____

V. Formatting slide backgrounds [PPT 95]

Fill is ______________________________

Solid fill is ______________________________

Gradient fill is ______________________________

Picture or texture fill uses ______________________________

Transparency allows ______________________________

Offsets are used to ______________________________

Tiling options repeat ______________________________

☞ To insert a texture fill

1. ______________________________
2. ______________________________
   ____
3. ______________________________
4. ______________________________

☞ To insert a picture to create a background

1. ______________________________
   ____
   ____
   ____
   ____
2. ______________________________

☞ To format the background picture fill transparency

The Transparency slider indicates ______________________________

____

1. ______________________________

☞ To format the background texture fill transparency

1. ______________________________
   ____
2. ______________________________

☞ To choose a background style

PowerPoint provides 12 background styles with designs that may include ______________________________

____

Fill effects add ______________________________

1. ______________________________
   ____
   ____
   ____
2. ______________________________

VI. Formatting title and content text [PPT 101]

The Format Painter allows you to ____________________

____

☞ To change the subtitle and caption font

1. ____________________
2. ____________________
3. ____________________
4. ____________________

____

____

☞ To shadow text

A shadow helps ____________________

1. ____________________

A. Format Painter [PPT 105]

You can use the Format Painter in three ways:

- ____________________
- ____________________
- ____________________

☞ To format text using the Format Painter

1. ____________________

____

2. ____________________

VII. Adding and formatting a shape [PPT 106]

☞ To add a shape

1. ____________________
2. ____________________

____

3. ____________________

☞ To resize a shape

1. ____________________
2. ____________________

____

☞ To copy and paste a shape

1. ____________________

2. ______________________________

☞ To add other shapes

1. ______________________________
2. ______________________________
3. ______________________________
4. ______________________________
5. ______________________________

☞ To apply a shape style

1. ______________________________
2. ______________________________
3. ______________________________

☞ To add formatted text to a shape

1. ______________________________

VIII. Using WordArt [PPT 113]

WordArt allows you to______________________________

The WordArt outline is ______________________________

An effect helps ______________________________

☞ To insert WordArt

1. ______________________________
2. ______________________________
3. ______________________________

☞ To change the WordArt shape

1. ______________________________

2. ______________________________

____

3. ______________________________

4. ______________________________

____

☞ To apply a WordArt text fill

1. ______________________________

____

2. ______________________________

☞ To change the weight of the WordArt outline

PowerPoint gives you the option to change the line weight, or thickness, starting with ¼ point and increasing in ¼ point increments.

1. ______________________________

____

____

____

2. ______________________________

☞ To change the color of the WordArt outline

1. ______________________________

____

____

2. ______________________________

Review

Matching (5)

Match each term on the left with the best description from the right.

___ 1. offset
___ 2. tiling
___ 3. transparency
___ 4. gradient
___ 5. solid fill

a. allows you to see through the background
b. often used as fill colors on graphs and as shadows
c. changes to the Followed Hyperlink color when you click the hyperlink text during a presentation
d. used to move the background from the slide borders in varying distances by percentages
e. kind of fill that is one color shade gradually progressing to another shade of the same color or one color progressing to another color
f. one color used throughout an entire slide
g. repeats the background image many times vertically and horizontally on the slide

True-False (5)

*Circle **T** if the statement is true and **F** if the statement is false.*

T F 1. You have permission to use the clips from the Microsoft Clip Organizer.

T F 2. The larger the tiling percentage, the greater number of times the image is repeated.

T F 3. Formatting text in a shape follows the same techniques as formatting text in a placeholder.

T F 4. Some WordArt styles can detract from the message you are trying to present if not used carefully.

T F 5. The weight of the lines that make up WordArt outlines are measured in picas.

Modified True-False (5)

*Circle **T** if the statement is true. If the statement is <u>false</u>, circle **F** and make the statement true by writing the replacement for the underlined word or phrase in the blank.*

T F 1. <u>Contrast</u> determines the overall lightness or darkness of an entire image.

____

T F 2. PowerPoint provides more than <u>125</u> picture styles that enable you easily to change a picture's look to a more visually appealing style.

____

T F 3. The <u>Opacity</u> slider indicates the amount of opaqueness.

____

T F 4. A WordArt <u>effect</u> helps add emphasis or depth to the characters.

____

T F 5. <u>Gradient</u> fill is one color used throughout the entire slide.

____

Definitions (5)

Briefly define each term.

1. gradient fill ______________________________
2. transparency ______________________________
3. Format Painter ______________________________
4. shadow ______________________________
5. WordArt ______________________________

The PowerPoint Screen (5)

Identify the elements indicated in Figure PPT3.

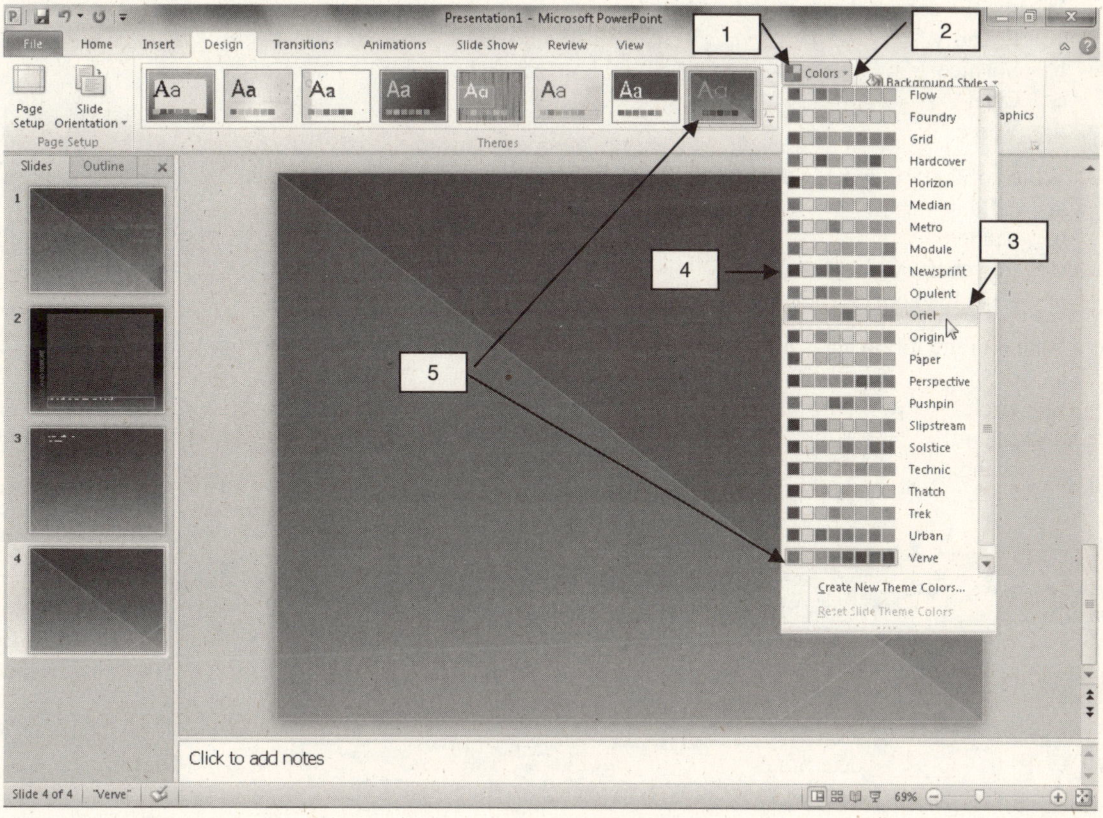

Figure PPT3

1. ______________________
2. ______________________
3. ______________________
4. ______________________
5. ______________________

Multiple Choice (5)

Circle the letter of the best answer.

1. What is the term for the content that makes up the interior of a shape, line, or character?
   a. base
   b. texture
   c. fill
   d. matter

2. How many background styles does PowerPoint provide for each theme?
   a. 6
   b. 12
   c. 18
   d. 24

3. What is the default theme in PowerPoint?
   a. Foundry
   b. Solstice
   c. Oriel
   d. Verve

4. Which of the following is a shape element provided by PowerPoint?
   a. callout
   b. banner
   c. flowchart symbol
   d. all of the above

5. Which of the following is *not* a geometric shape included in the Shapes gallery?
   a. orb
   b. circle
   c. square
   d. triangle

Dialog Box (5)

Answer the following questions about the Format Background dialog box shown in Figure PPT4.

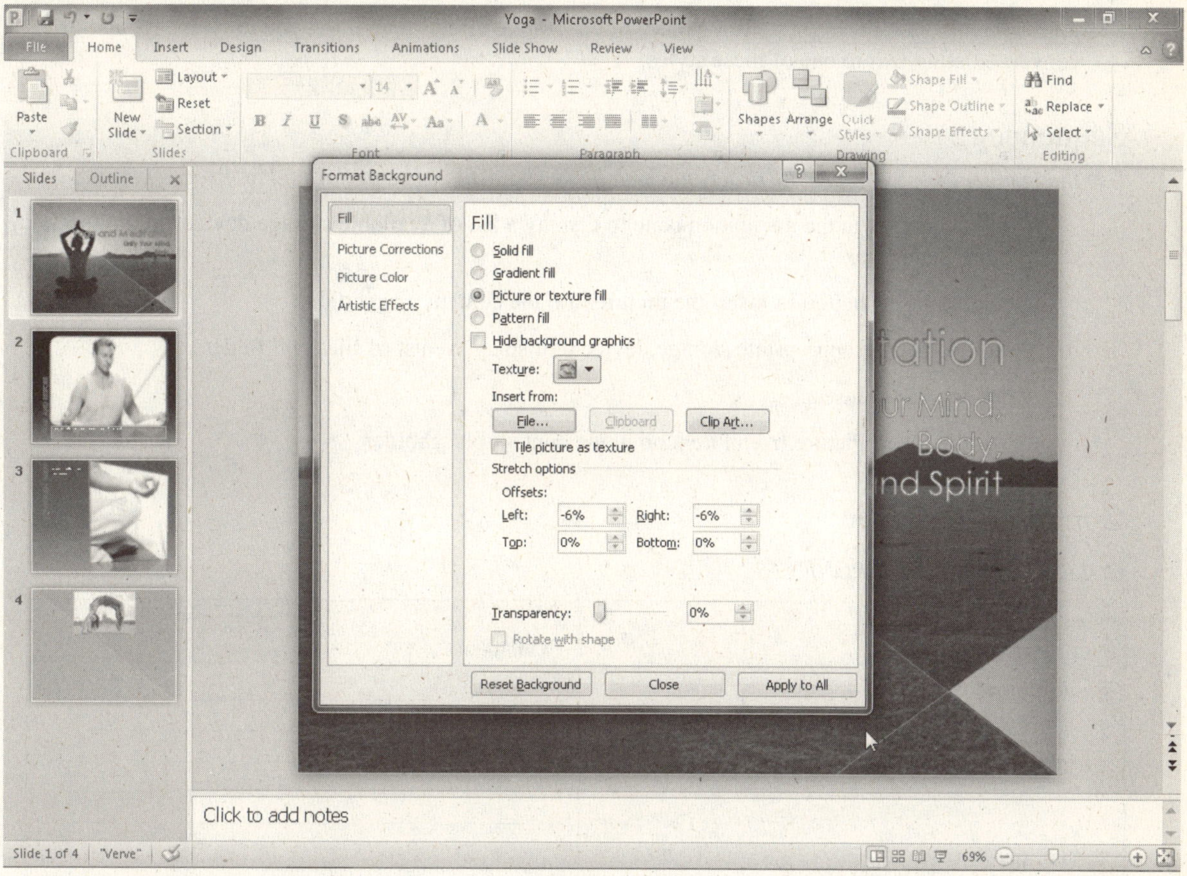

Figure PPT4

1. How was the dialog box displayed? ______________________________
2. How do you move the Transparency slider in small increments? ______________________________
3. Why do the Left and Right offsets in the Stretch options area show their current values? ______________________________
4. How can you move the dialog box so you can see more of the subtitle text behind it? ______________________________
5. What is the default transparency value? ______________________________

Fill in the Blanks (5)

Write a word (or words) in the blank to complete each sentence correctly.

1. ____________________ is the difference between the darkest and lightest areas of the image.
2. Picture or ____________________ fill uses a specific file or an image that simulates a material, such as cork, granite, marble, or canvas.
3. ____________________ effects add patterns and texture to a background.

4. With WordArt outlines, PowerPoint gives you the option to change the line ________________________, or thickness, starting with ¼ point and increasing in ¼ point increments.
5. ________________________ is a gallery of decorative effects that allow you to type new text or convert existing text to one of these styles.

Sequence (5)

Use the numbers 1 – 5 to show the order in which these steps should be performed to insert a picture.

___ Click Computer in the navigation pane to display a list of available storage devices in the Insert Picture dialog box.

___ Click the Insert button to insert the picture into the content placeholder.

___ Double-click the appropriate storage device to display the list of files and folders.

___ Click the file to insert.

___ Click the Insert Picture from File icon in the content placeholder.

Complete the Table

COLOR SCHEME COMPONENTS

Components	Description
Background color	
Text color	
Accent colors	
Hyperlink colors	

Short Answer (5)

Write a brief answer to each question.

1. What is a style?

2. What are some examples of picture effects provided by PowerPoint?

3. How do you insert a background on all slides in a presentation simultaneously?

4. How do you remove a shadow from text?

5. What are the three ways in which you can use the Format Painter feature?

Activities

Expanding on Apply Your Knowledge

Perform the following tasks.

1. Open the Apply 2-1 Chemistry Lab Safety presentation created in Apply Your Knowledge.
2. Change the background style to a style of your choosing.
3. Change the title text font size to 64 point, change the font to Garamond, and change the font color to Green. Change the font color of your name to an appropriate color.
4. On Slide 2, exchange the photographs in Figure 2-74b on page PPT 124 with other appropriate photographs.
5. Move Slide 3 to become the new Slide 2 using Slide Sorter view.
6. Change the slide transitions used to transitions of your choosing.
7. Print the revised presentation.
8. Save the revised presentation as Apply 2-1 Chemistry Lab Safety_WKBK.

Expanding on the Lab

Perform the following tasks.

1. Open the Lab 2-1 Trip to Germany presentation created in In the Lab 1.
2. On slides 2, 3, 4, and 5, apply the Style 5 background style. Change the layout of slides 2 and 3 from Two Content to another layout.
3. On slides 4 and 5, change the color of the title text to another color and change the font size to 30.
4. Change the colors of the picture borders in slides 3, 4, and 5 to Red.
5. Check the presentation for errors.
6. Print the revised presentation handout. Print the revised black and white presentation.
7. Save the revised presentation as Lab 2-1 Trip to Germany_WKBK.

Microsoft PowerPoint 2010

Chapter Three
Reusing a Presentation and Adding Media

Overview

In this chapter, you learn how to enhance an existing presentation by adding video, audio, and pictures with effects. You also learn how to modify placeholders, align text, and review a presentation by checking spelling and creating handouts.

Chapter Outline

I. Introduction [PPT 138]

II. Project — Presentation with Video, Audio, and Pictures with Effects [PPT 138]

A. Overview [PPT 138]

The general guidelines to follow when creating a presentation with illustrations are

1. ____

____

2. ____

3. ____

____

4. ____

____

5. ____

____

III. Starting PowerPoint [PPT 140]

☞ To start PowerPoint and open and save a presentation

1. ____

2. ____

3. ____

4. ____

IV. Inserting pictures and adding effects [PPT 141]

Color saturation changes ______________________________

Color tone affects ______________________________

A color cast occurs when ______

Recolor effects convert ______

Grayscale changes ______

Sepia changes ______

☞ To color a picture

1. ______
2. ______

______

______

☞ To add an artistic effect to a picture

1. ______
2. ______

______

______

☞ To change the stacking order

Bring Forward moves ______

Send Backward moves ______

Bring to Front moves ______

Send to Back moves ______

1. ______
2. ______
3. ______

______

V. Modifying placeholders and deleting a slide [PPT 148]

☞ To resize a placeholder

1. ______

______

☞ To move a placeholder

1. ______

______

______

☞ To align paragraph text

When you left-align a paragraph, it ______

When you right-align a paragraph, it ______

When text is justified, it ______

1. ______

2. ______________________________

3. ______________________________

4. ______________________________

5. ______________________________

☞ To delete a slide

1. ______________________________

2. ______________________________

A. Changing views [PPT 153]

☞ To change views

1. ______________________________

2. ______________________________

3. ______________________________

____

____

4. ______________________________

____

VI. Copying and modifying a clip [PPT 154]

The Office Clipboard is ______________________________

☞ To copy a clip from one slide to another

1. ______________________________

2. ______________________________

3. ______________________________

☞ To zoom a slide

1. ______________________________

☞ To ungroup a clip

When you ungroup a clip art picture, PowerPoint breaks ______________________________

____

1. ______________________________

____

2. ______________________________

3. ______________________________

____

____

☞ To change the color of a clip object

1. ______________________________
   ____
2. ______________________________
   ____
   ____
3. ______________________________
   ____
4. ______________________________
   ____
5. ______________________________
6. ______________________________
   ____
7. ______________________________

☞ To delete a clip object

1. ______________________________
2. ______________________________

☞ To regroup objects

1. ______________________________
   ____
2. ______________________________
3. ______________________________

VII. Adding media to slides [PPT 163]

☞ To insert a video file

1. ______________________________
   ____
   ____
2. ______________________________

☞ To trim a video file

PowerPoint's Trim Video feature allows you to ______________________________
____

1. ______________________________
   ____
2. ______________________________
   ____

3. ______________________________

____

☞ To add video options

Full screen means ______________________________

1. ______________________________
2. ______________________________
3. ______________________________

____

4. ______________________________

☞ To insert an audio file

1. ______________________________
2. ______________________________

____

____

3. ______________________________

____

A Windows waveform (.wav) file uses ______________________________

____

4. ______________________________
5. ______________________________
6. ______________________________
7. ______________________________

____

8. ______________________________

☞ To add audio options

1. ______________________________

____

2. ______________________________
3. ______________________________
4. ______________________________

☞ To add a video style

1. ______________________________
2. ______________________________

____

____

3. ______________________________

☞ To resize a video

1. ______________________________

____

2. ______________________________

☞ To insert a movie clip

1. ______________________________

____

____

____

2. ______________________________

____

____

VIII. Reviewing and revising individual slides [PPT 176]

A. Replace dialog box [PPT 176]

☞ To find and replace text

1. ______________________________

____

____

2. ______________________________

3. ______________________________

☞ To find and insert a synonym

A synonym is ______________________________

A thesaurus is ______________________________

1. ______________________________

____

2. ______________________________

An antonym is ______________________________

☞ To add notes

You can type and format notes in the Notes pane as you work in Normal view and then print this information as notes pages.

1. ______________________________

____

2. ______________________________

____

B. Checking spelling [PPT 180]

A custom dictionary is available if ______________________________

____

☞ To check spelling

1. ______________________________

____

2. ______________________________

____

3. ______________________________

____

☞ To insert a slide number

1. ______________________________

____

2. ______________________________

____

3. ______________________________

____

☞ To preview and print a handout

1. ______________________________

____

2. ______________________________

3. ______________________________

____

____

☞ To print speaker notes

1. ______________________________

2. ______________________________

____

3. ______________________________

____

Review

Matching (5)

Match each term on the left with the best description from the right.

___ 1. color saturation
___ 2. color cast
___ 3. recolor effects
___ 4. grayscale
___ 5. sepia

a. occurs when one color dominates a picture
b. has a wide variety of present formatting combinations
c. changes the intensity of colors
d. converts a picture into a wide variety of hues
e. reapplies a change reversed with the Undo button
f. changes picture colors into brown, gold, and yellow
g. changes a color picture into black, white, and shades of gray

True-False (5)

*Circle **T** if the statement is true and **F** if the statement is false.*

T F 1. The Move to Top command moves an object toward the top of the object stack.

T F 2. Designers use alignment within paragraphs to aid readability and to indicate relationships among slide elements.

T F 3. You may need to ungroup a complex object into less complex objects before being able to modify a specific object.

T F 4. Dragging or sizing affects only a selected object, not the entire collection of objects, so you must use caution when objects are not completely regrouped.

T F 5. An audio clip can play either automatically or when clicked.

Modified True-False (5)

*Circle **T** if the statement is true. If the statement is false, circle **F** and make the statement true by writing the replacement for the underlined word or phrase in the blank.*

T F 1. The Move to Top command moves a selected object to the top of the object stack.

____

T F 2. When you right-align a paragraph, the last character of the text line is near the right border.

____

T F 3. A(n) homonym is a word similar in meaning to another.

____

T F 4. A(n) master dictionary is available if you want to add special words such as proper names, cities, and acronyms.

____

T F 5. You can type and format notes in the Notes pane as you work in Normal view and then print this information as notes pages.

____

Definitions (5)

Briefly define each term.

1. Office Clipboard ____________________
2. ungroup ____________________
3. thesaurus ____________________
4. Trim Video ____________________
5. full screen ____________________

The PowerPoint Screen (5)

Identify the elements indicated in Figure PPT5.

Figure PPT5

1. ____________________
2. ____________________
3. ____________________
4. ____________________
5. ____________________

Multiple Choice (5)

Circle the letter of the best answer.

1. What key do you press and hold while dragging a sizing handle away from or toward the center of a picture to maintain its proportions?
   a. TAB
   b. F1
   c. SHIFT
   d. ALT

2. Which of the following recolor effects changes a picture's color in brown, gold, and yellow?
   a. grayscale
   b. sepia
   c. antique
   d. historical

3. Which of the following commands moves an object underneath another object?
   a. Send Backward
   b. Bring to Front
   c. Move Under
   d. Send to Back

4. Which view displays each slide individually without the slides filling the entire screen?
   a. Slide Show
   b. Slide Sorter
   c. Reading
   d. Outline

5. Which of the following encodes and communicates music and sound between computers, music synthesizers, and instruments?
   a. .gif
   b. .wav
   c. .png
   d. .mpeg

Dialog Box (5)

Answer the following questions about the Trim Video dialog box shown in Figure PPT6.

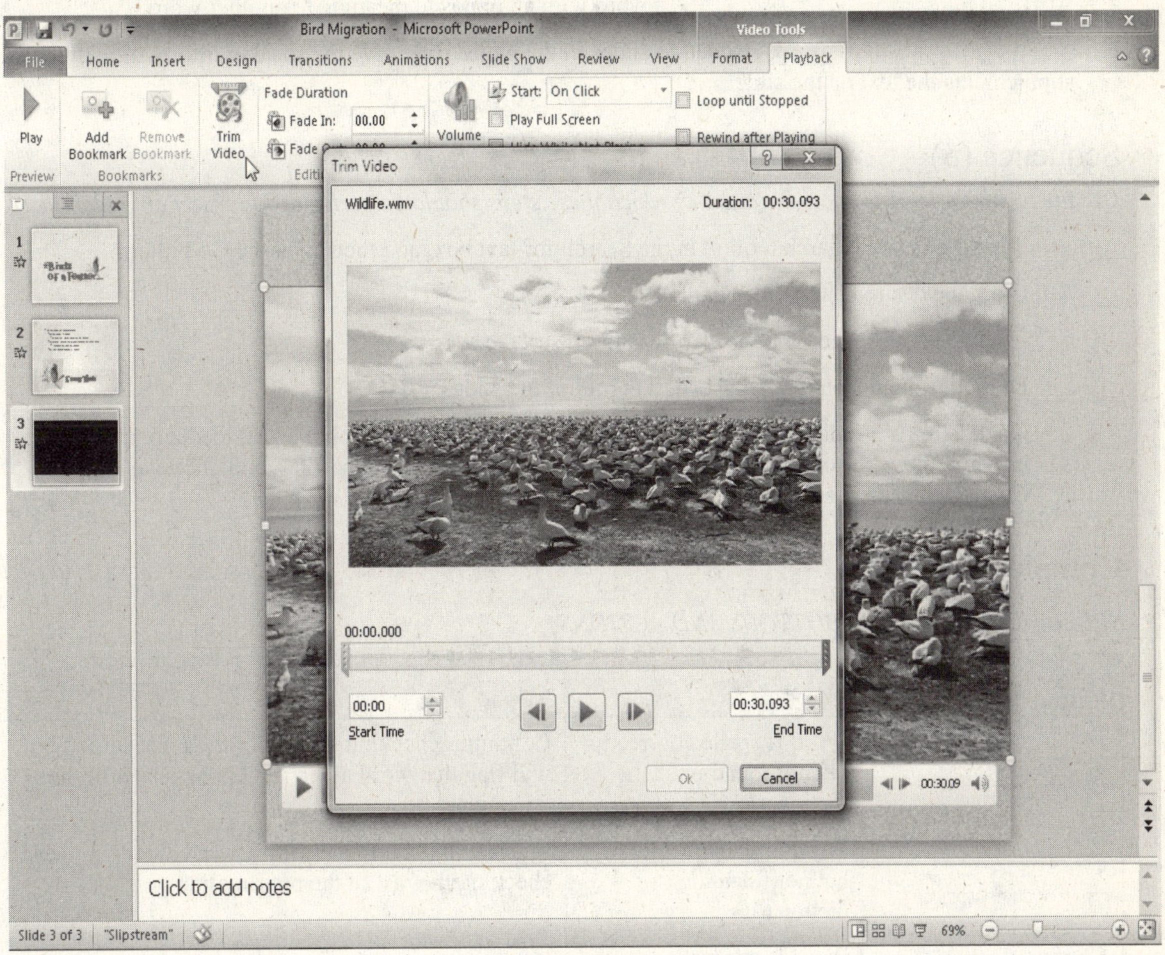

Figure PPT6

1. How was the dialog box displayed? ______________________
2. What does this feature allow you to do? ______________________
____
3. What happens when you click the Play button? ______________________
4. Can you specify the start or end times without dragging the markers?______________________
____
5. How would you indicate an end point if you wanted the clip to end at a time other than at the end of the clip?______________________

Fill in the Blanks (5)

Write a word (or words) in the blank to complete each sentence correctly.

1. The ______________ command moves the selected object underneath all objects on a slide.
2. A paragraph can be ______________ so that the text is aligned to both the left and right borders.

3. PowerPoint classifies ________________________ files as a type of video or movie because the clips have movement or action.
4. A(n) ________________________ is a word with an opposite meaning to another word.
5. ________________________ added to slides in the Notes pane give the speaker information that supplements the text on the slide.

Sequence (5)

Use the numbers 1 – 5 to show the order in which these steps should be performed to insert an audio file.

___ Type the desired search term(s) in the Search for text box, and then click the Go button.

___ Click the desired clip in the results list.

___ Click the Insert Audio button arrow on the Insert tab.

___ Drag the sound icon to the upper-left corner of the slide.

___ Click Clip Art Audio, click the 'Results should be' box arrow, click the 'All media types' check box to remove the check mark from each of the four types of media files, and click the Audio check box.

Complete the Table

SPELLING DIALOG BOX BUTTONS AND ACTIONS

Button Name	When to Use	Action
________________	Word is spelled correctly but not found in dictionaries	Continues checking the rest of the presentation but will flag that word again if it appears later in the document.
________________	Word is spelled correctly but not found in dictionaries	Ignores all occurrences of the word and continues checking the rest of the presentation.
Change	Word is misspelled	________________ ________________ ________________
Change All	Word is misspelled	________________ ________________ ________________
Add	Add word to custom dictionary	________________ ________________ ________________
Suggest	________________ ________________	Lists alternative spellings. Click the correct word from the Suggestions box or type the proper spelling. Corrects the word and continues checking the rest of the presentation.
AutoCorrect	________________ ________________	PowerPoint adds the spelling error and its correction to the AutoCorrect list. Any future misspelling of the word is corrected automatically as you type.

Short Answer (5)

Write a brief answer to each question.

1. How do square sizing handles differ from circle sizing handles?

2. Can you open the Microsoft Clip Organizer when you are not using PowerPoint? If so, how do you do it?

3. What is a codec used for?

4. What are the two options in the Replace dialog box that are useful when revising slides?

5. In what way can handouts be useful to help you organize your speech?

Activities

Expanding on Make It Right

Perform the following tasks.

1. Open the Make It Right 3-1 Chilean Flamingos presentation created in Make It Right.
2. On Slide 1, change the audio clip volume to Medium, and use the Play across slides option.
3. On Slide 2, add the Bevel Perspective video effect to the video.
4. On Slide 3, ungroup the flamingo clip and then recolor the three circular shapes that make up the water at the flamingo's feet to a shade of blue. Regroup the clip.
5. On Slide 3, add a 3 pt Green border to the picture.
6. In the Slide 1 Notes page, add the following sentence: "Baby flamingos are gray in color, but by adulthood their plumage color ranges from pink to red."
7. Print the revised presentation.
8. Save the revised presentation as Make It Right 3-1 Chilean Flamingos_WKBK.

Expanding on the Lab

Perform the following tasks.

1. Open the Lab 3-1 Cooking presentation created in In the Lab 1.
2. On Slide 1, change the volume of the audio clip to High.
3. On Slide 2, change the weight of the picture border to 3 pt, and change the color of the border to Green.
4. On Slide 4, apply the Mosaic Bubbles artistic effect to the lobster picture in the left content placeholder. Change the color of the paella picture in the right content placeholder to Blue, Accent color 1 Light (Recolor area).
5. On Slide 4, insert an audio clip of your choosing from Office.com. Start the clip automatically, play across slides, and hide the sound icon during the show.
6. On Slide 5, move the sound icon to the lower-left corner of the slide, and change the Playback option to Loop until Stopped.
7. Review the slides in Slide Sorter view to check for consistency. Then click the Reading view button to display the current slide, and click the Next and Previous buttons to display each slide. Change the view to Normal.
8. Save the revised presentation as Lab 3-1 Cooking_WKBK.

Microsoft Excel 2010

Chapter One
Creating a Worksheet and an Embedded Chart

Overview

In this chapter, you learn how to enter text and numbers to create a worksheet. The chapter also illustrates how to select a range, use the Sum button, format cells, insert a chart, and preview and print a worksheet.

Chapter Outline

I. Introduction [EX 2]

An Excel worksheet allows ______________________________

A chart conveys ______________________________

The process of developing a worksheet that communicates specific information requires careful analysis and planning. The steps in the process of developing a worksheet include:

- ______________________________
- ______________________________
- ______________________________
- ______________________________

II. Project — Worksheet with an Embedded Chart [EX 2]

A requirements document includes ______________________________

A. Overview [EX 4]

☞ To start Excel

1. ______________________________
2. ______________________________
3. ______________________________
4. ______________________________

III. Selecting a cell [EX 7]

To enter data into a cell, you first must select it.

To select a cell, either:

- Use the mouse to ______________________________
- Press an arrow key to ______________________________

IV. Entering text [EX 7]

In Excel, text is ______________________________

☞ To enter the worksheet titles

1. ______________________________

2. ______________________________

Clicking the Enter box ______________________________

Clicking the Cancel box ______________________________

The insertion point is ______________________________

3. ______________________________

4. ______________________________

____

____

A. AutoCorrect [EX 9]

The AutoCorrect feature works ______________________________

____

AutoCorrect makes three types of corrections:

1. ______________________________

2. ______________________________

3. ______________________________

☞ To enter column titles

1. ______________________________

2. ______________________________

3. ______________________________

4. ______________________________

☞ To enter row titles

1. ______________________________

____

2. ______________________________

V. Entering numbers [EX 13]

A number can contain ______________________________

☞ To enter numbers

1. ______________________________

2. ______________________________

3. ______________________________

____

VI. Calculating a sum [EX 15]

The SUM function adds ______

A range is ______

______

☞ To sum a column of numbers

1. ______

______

2. ______

VII. Using the fill handle to copy a cell to adjacent cells [EX 16]

The source area (copy area) is ______

The destination area (paste area) is ______

When you copy cell references, Excel adjusts them for each new position.

A relative reference is ______

☞ To copy a cell to adjacent cells in a row

The fill handle is ______

1. ______

2. ______

3. ______

☞ To determine multiple totals at the same time

1. ______

2. ______

3. ______

VIII. Formatting the worksheet [EX 20]

You format a worksheet to emphasize ______

______

A. Font, style, size, and color [EX 22]

Font (font face) defines ______

Font style indicates ______

Font size specifies ______

Point size is used to measure the height of a character. A single point ≈ ______

Font color defines ______

☞ To change a cell style

1. ______

______

2. ______

3. ______________________________

____

☞ To change the font

1. ______________________________

____

2. ______________________________

____

A theme is ______________________________

3. ______________________________

☞ To bold a cell

You bold an entry in a cell to ______________________________

1. ______________________________

☞ To increase the font size of a cell entry

1. ______________________________

____

2. ______________________________

☞ To change the font color of a cell entry

1. ______________________________

____

2. ______________________________

☞ To center a cell entry across columns by merging cells

Merging cells involves ______________________________

1. ______________________________

2. ______________________________

3. ______________________________

The opposite of merging cells is ______________________________

☞ To format column titles and the total row

1. ______________________________

2. ______________________________

____

3. ______________________________

____

____

4. ______________________________

____

☞ To format numbers in the worksheet

1. ______________________________
2. ______________________________
____
3. ______________________________
____
4. ______________________________
____

☞ To adjust the column width

1. ______________________________
2. ______________________________

IX. Using the Name box to select a cell [EX 34]

☞ To use the Name box to select a cell

1. ______________________________
2. ______________________________

A. Other ways to select cells [EX 35]

Excel supports several additional ways to select a cell.

X. Adding a clustered cylinder chart to the worksheet [EX 36]

An embedded chart is ______________________________

The y-axis or value axis (vertical axis) scale is ______________________________

☞ To add a clustered cylinder chart to the worksheet

1. ______________________________
2. ______________________________
3. ______________________________
4. ______________________________
____
5. ______________________________
____

The x-axis (horizontal axis), or category axis, titles are ______________________________

6. ______________________________
____

Holding down the ALT key while you drag a chart ______________________________

7. ______________________________
____

8. ____________________

The legend identifies ____________________

XI. Changing the worksheet names [EX 42]

☞ To change the worksheet names

The Document Information Panel contains ____________________

1. ____________________

____

2. ____________________

____

3. ____________________

4. ____________________

XII. Changing document properties and saving again [EX 43]

Document properties (metadata) are ____________________

A keyword is ____________________

Standard properties are ____________________

Automatically updated properties include ____________________

____

☞ To change document properties

The Document Information Panel contains ____________________

1. ____________________

2. ____________________

3. ____________________

4. ____________________

____

____

____

☞ To save an existing document with the same file name

1. ____________________

____

XIII. Previewing and printing a worksheet [EX 45]

A hard copy (printout) is ____________________

Printed copies of your document can be useful for the following reasons:

- ____________________
- ____________________

Green computing is ____________________

☞ To preview and print a worksheet in landscape orientation

1. ______________________________

____

2. ______________________________
3. ______________________________
4. ______________________________

☞ To quit Excel

1. ______________________________
2. ______________________________

XIV. Starting Excel and opening a workbook [EX 47]

☞ To open a workbook from Excel

1. ______________________________
2. ______________________________
3. ______________________________
4. ______________________________
5. ______________________________

XV. AutoCalculate [EX 48]

The AutoCalculate area can be used to obtain information about numbers in a range.

☞ To use the AutoCalculate area to determine a maximum

1. ______________________________
2. ______________________________

____

3. ______________________________

XVI. Correcting errors [EX 49]

You can correct errors on a worksheet using several methods.

A. Correcting errors while you are typing data into a cell [EX 49]

If you notice an error while typing data into a cell, press ______________________________

____

B. Correcting errors after entering data into a cell [EX 50]

If you find an error after entering the data into a cell, you can correct the error in one of two ways:

1. If the entry is short, select ______________________________

____

2. If the entry is long and errors are minor, double-click the cell to switch to Edit mode.

(a) In-cell editing is ____________________

____

(b) Make your changes.

(1) To insert characters, place ____________________

____

(2) To delete characters, move ____________________

____

____

(3) When you are finished, click ____________________

The INSERT key toggles the keyboard between Insert mode and Overtype mode.

In Insert mode, Excel inserts ____________________

In Overtype mode, Excel overtypes ____________________

C. Undoing the last cell entry [EX 51]

The Undo command on the Quick Access Toolbar can be used ____________________

D. Clearing a cell or range of cells [EX 52]

☞ To clear cell entries using the fill handle

1. ____________________

2. ____________________

☞ To clear cell entries using the shortcut menu

1. ____________________

2. ____________________

3. ____________________

☞ To clear cell entries using the DELETE key

1. ____________________

2. ____________________

☞ To clear cell entries and formatting using the Clear button

1. ____________________

2. ____________________

3. ____________________

☞ To clear formatting using the Cell Styles button

1. ____________________

2. ____________________

3. ____________________

Never press the SPACEBAR to ____________________

E. Clearing the entire worksheet [EX 52]

☞ To clear the entire worksheet

1. ______________________________

2. ______________________________

☞ To delete an embedded chart

1. ______________________________

2. ______________________________

Review

Matching (5)

Match each key or key combination on the left with the best description from the right.

___ 1. ALT+PAGE DOWN

___ 2. CTRL+ARROW

___ 3. CTRL+HOME

___ 4. HOME

___ 5. PAGE DOWN

a. selects the cell one window to the right and moves the window accordingly

b. selects cell A1 or the cell one column and one row below and to the right of frozen titles and moves the window accordingly

c. selects the cell one window to the left and moves the window accordingly

d. selects the border cell of the worksheet in combination with the arrow keys and moves the window accordingly

e. selects the cell up one window from the active cell and moves the window accordingly

f. selects the cell at the beginning of the row that contains the active cell and moves the window accordingly

g. selects the cell down one window from the active cell and moves the window accordingly

True-False (5)

*Circle **T** if the statement is true and **F** if the statement is false.*

T F 1. The key to developing a useful worksheet is careful planning.

T F 2. Worksheet titles and subtitles should be as brief and meaningful as possible.

T F 3. When you begin typing a cell entry, Excel displays two additional boxes in the formula bar: the Cancel box and the Display box.

T F 4. With Excel in Edit mode, you can edit the contents directly in the cell—a procedure called inline editing.

T F 5. Press the SPACEBAR to clear a selected cell.

Modified True-False (5)

*Circle **T** if the statement is true. If the statement is false, circle **F** and make the statement true by writing the replacement for the underlined word or phrase in the blank.*

T F 1. When you copy cell references, Excel automatically adjusts them for each new location; each adjusted cell reference is called a(n) destination reference.

____

T F 2. Clicking the Display box completes the entry you have typed in a cell.

____

T F 3. You format a worksheet to emphasize certain entries and make the worksheet easier to read and understand.

____

T F 4. Font theme indicates how the characters are emphasized.

____

T F 5. When you are proposing a range to sum, Excel first looks for a range of cells with numbers above the active cell and then to the right.

____

Definitions (5)

Briefly define each term.

1. radar chart ______________________________
2. cell ______________________________
3. range ______________________________
4. legend ______________________________
5. embedded chart ______________________________

The Excel Screen (5)

Identify the elements indicated in Figure EX1.

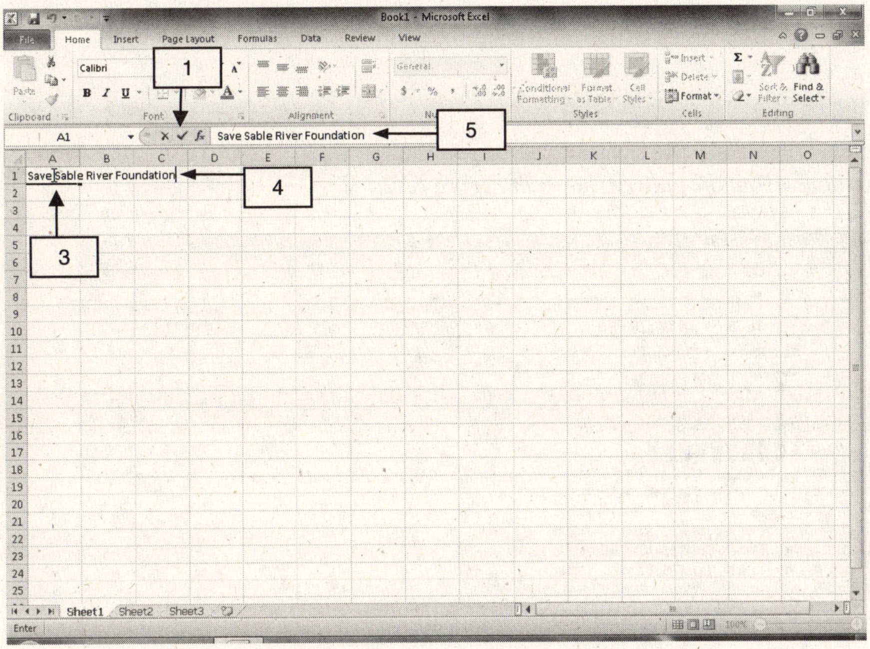

Figure EX1

1. ______________________________
2. ______________________________
3. ______________________________
4. ______________________________
5. ______________________________

Multiple Choice (5)

Circle the letter of the best answer.

1. Which of the following is not a type of correction AutoCorrect can make for you?
   a. correcting two initial capital letters by changing the second letter to lowercase
   b. capitalizing the first letter in the names of days
   c. capitalizing the first letter in proper names
   d. replacing commonly misspelled words with their correct spelling

2. Which of the following are you required to enter?
   a. commas
   b. dollar signs
   c. trailing zeroes
   d. none of the above

3. When using the SUM function, how can you enter the correct range by typing?
   a. type the beginning cell reference, a hyphen (-), and the ending cell reference
   b. type the beginning cell reference, a colon (:), and the ending cell reference
   c. type the beginning cell reference, a slash (/), and the ending cell reference
   d. type the beginning cell reference, an asterisk (*), and the ending cell reference

4. Which of the following cannot be contained in a number?
   a. +
   b. $
   c. *
   d. e

5. Which of the following is an alternative to clicking the Select All button?
   a. CTRL+A
   b. ALT+S
   c. CTRL+S
   d. ALT+A

Gallery (5)

Answer the following questions about the gallery shown in Figure EX2.

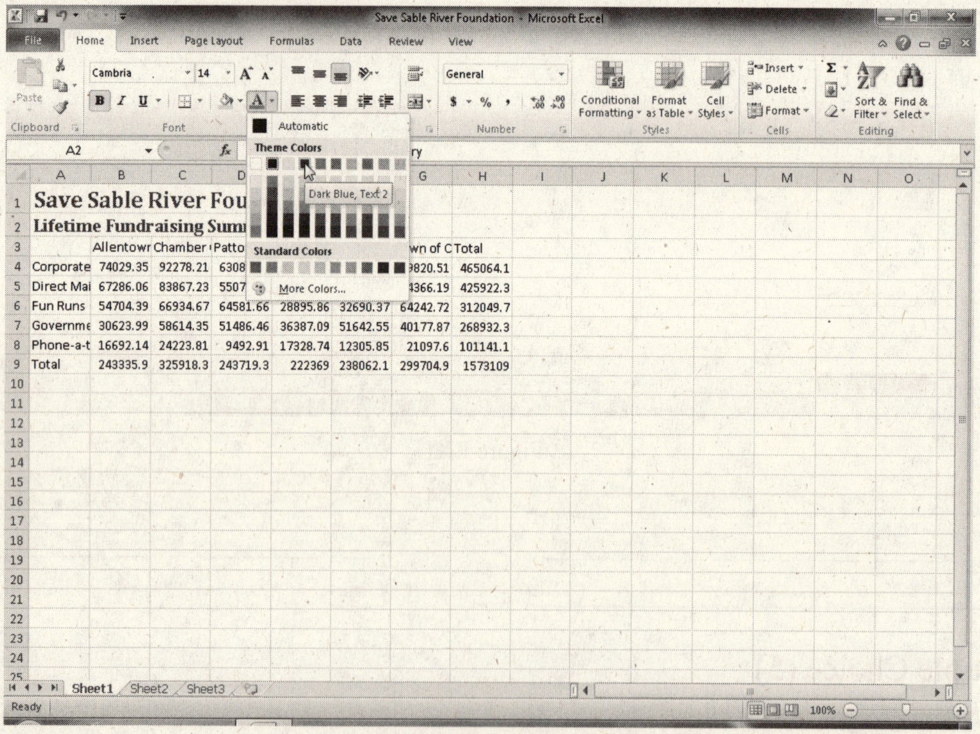

Figure EX2

1. What is live preview? ______________________________

2. Which colors does Excel make available on this gallery? ______________________________
____

3. What happens to the Font Color button after you select the new font color? ____________________
____

4. How do you display the gallery shown? ____________________________________

5. How can you use the Mini toolbar to display the gallery? ____________________________
____

Fill in the Blanks (5)

Write a word (or words) in the blank to complete each sentence correctly.

1. In ______________________ mode, Excel overtypes, or replaces, the character to the right of the insertion point.
2. The easiest way to ______________________ a cell (make it active) is to use the mouse to move the block plus sign to the cell and then click.
3. To cancel an entire entry before entering it into a cell, click the Cancel box in the formula bar or press the ______________________.
4. A character with a(n) ______________________ of 10 is about 10/72 of one inch in height.
5. Holding down the ALT key while you drag a chart ______________________ (aligns) the edge of the chart area to the worksheet gridlines.

Sequence (5)

Use the numbers 1 – 5 to show the order in which these steps should be performed to add a clustered cylinder chart to a worksheet.

___ Select the cell range.

___ Click the clustered cylinder chart type in the Cylinder area of the Column gallery.

___ Click the Insert tab.

___ Click the Column button on the Ribbon.

___ Position and resize the chart as desired.

Complete the Table

SUMMARY OF IN-CELL EDITING TASKS

Task	Mouse	Keyboard
Move the insertion point to the beginning of data in a cell.	____________________ ____________________	Press HOME
____________________ ____________________	Position the mouse pointer to the right of the last character and click.	Press END
Move the insertion point anywhere in a cell.	____________________ ____________________	Press RIGHT ARROW or LEFT ARROW
____________________ ____________________	Drag the mouse pointer through adjacent characters.	Press SHIFT+RIGHT ARROW or SHIFT+LEFT ARROW

Select all data in a cell.	____________________ ____________________	
____________________ ____________________	Click the Cut button on the Home tab on the Ribbon.	Press DELETE
Delete characters to the left of the insertion point.		____________________
____________________ ____________________		Press DELETE
Toggle between Insert and Overtype modes.		____________________

Short Answer (5)

Write a brief answer to each question.

1. What is the difference between standard document properties and automatically updated properties?

2. What does the AutoFill Options button do?

3. Which fonts are displayed in the Font gallery?

4. How do you choose the type of chart you need?

5. For what reasons can hard copies be useful?

Activities

Expanding on the Case

Perform the following tasks.

1. Open the worksheet created in Cases and Places 1.
2. Reformat the column headings as 16-point Helvetica bold.
3. Change 3rd Quarter Copies and Supplies expenses to $95.
4. Change Miscellaneous expenses for the 4th Quarter to $56.
5. Change 2nd Quarter Travel expenses to $625.
6. Reformat the table range using a new format.
7. Change the chart type from clustered cylinder to another type.
8. Print the modified worksheet.
9. Save the workbook as Travel Club Expenses_WKBK.

Expanding on the Lab

Perform the following tasks.

1. Open the Lab 1-1 A Healthy Body Shop Annual Revenue Analysis worksheet created in In the Lab 1.
2. Reformat the worksheet title, A Healthy Body Shop, as 24-point Book Antiqua bold.
3. Change Aquatics for Phoenix to $92,115.23.
4. Change Dance for Atlanta to $69,051.43.
5. Change Weight Training for New York to $76,882.24.
6. Reformat the range B4:G9 using a new format.
7. Move the chart so that two more rows display between the chart and the table.
8. Print the modified worksheet.
9. Save the workbook as Lab 1-1 A Healthy Body Shop Annual Revenue Analysis_WKBK.

Microsoft Excel 2010

Chapter Two
Formulas, Functions, and Formatting

Overview

In creating the workbook in this chapter, you learn how to enter formulas, calculate an average, find the highest and lowest numbers in a range, verify formulas using Range Finder, add borders, align text, format numbers, change column widths and row heights, and add conditional formatting to a range of numbers. In addition, you learn how to spell check a worksheet, print a section of a worksheet, and display and print the formulas version of the worksheet using the Fit to option.

Chapter Outline

I. Introduction [EX 66]

A function is ______________________________

II. Project — Worksheet with Formulas and Functions [EX 66]

A. Overview [EX 68]

III. Entering the titles and numbers into the worksheet [EX 71]

IV. Entering formulas [EX 74]

One of the reasons Excel is a valuable tool is that you can ______________________________

A circular reference is ______________________________

Functions are ______________________________

Arguments are ______________________________

☞ To enter a formula using the keyboard

1. ______________________________

The equal sign (=) alerts ______________________________

The asterisk (*) directs Excel to ______________________________

2. ______________________________

A. Arithmetic operations [EX 76]

Valid arithmetic operators include:			
–	______________	/	______________
%	______________	+	______________
^	______________	–	______________
*	______________		

B. Order of operations [EX 77]

Moving from left to right in a formula, the order of operations is ____________________

____

You can use parentheses to override ______________________________

☞ To enter formulas using Point mode

Point mode allows ____________________________________

1. ____

2. ____

3. ____

____

4. ____

____

5. ____

____

☞ To copy formulas using the fill handle

1. ____

____

2. ____

____

Relative cell references are ______________________________

C. Option buttons [EX 82]

Several option buttons are available in Excel such as AutoCorrect, AutoFill, error checking, and others.

V. Using the AVERAGE, MAX, and MIN functions [EX 84]

You can enter functions using one of five methods:

1. ____

2. ____

3. ____

4. ____

5. ____

☞ To determine the average of a range of numbers using the keyboard and mouse

The AVERAGE function sums ______________________________

____

1. ______________________________

____

____

2. ______________________________

____

3. ______________________________

☞ To determine the highest number in a range of numbers using the Insert Function box

The MAX function displays ______________________________

1. ______________________________

____

____

2. ______________________________

____

3. ______________________________

☞ To determine the lowest number in a range of numbers using the Sum menu

The MIN function determines ______________________________

1. ______________________________

____

2. ______________________________

3. ______________________________

4. ______________________________

☞ To copy a range of cells across columns to an adjacent range using the fill handle

1. ______________________________

____

2. ______________________________

3. ______________________________

VI. Verifying formulas using Range Finder [EX 91]

Range Finder can be used to check ______________________________

____

☞ To verify a formula using Range Finder

1. ______________________________

2. ______________________________

VII. Formatting the worksheet [EX 92]

☞ To change the workbook theme

1. ______________________________

____

2. ______________________________

☞ To change the background and apply a box border to the worksheet title and subtitle

1. ______________________________

2. ______________________________

3. ______________________________

4. ______________________________

____

☞ To format dates and center data in cells

1. ______________________________

____

____

2. ______________________________

3. ______________________________

____

A. Formatting numbers using the Ribbon [EX 100]

The Accounting number format displays ______________________________

____

A fixed dollar sign displays ______________________________

A floating dollar sign appears ______________________________

The Comma style format inserts ______________________________

____

☞ To apply an Accounting style format and Comma style format using the Ribbon

1. ______________________________

____

____

2. ______________________________

____

3. ______________________________

____

____

☞ To apply a Currency style format with a floating dollar sign using the Format Cells dialog box

1. ______________________________

____

2. ______________________________

____

3. ______________________________

☞ To apply a Percent style format and use the Increase Decimal button

1. ______________________________

____

2. ______________________________

B. Conditional formatting [EX 104]

Conditional formatting is ______________________________

____

A condition is ______________________________

☞ To apply conditional formatting

1. ______________________________

____

2. ______________________________

____

____

____

3. ______________________________

____

4. ______________________________

5. ______________________________

____

C. Conditional formatting operators [EX 107]

There are eight different relational operators from which you can choose for conditional formatting in the New Formatting Rule dialog box.

D. Changing the width of columns and heights of rows [EX 107]

A pixel is ______________________________

☞ To change the width of columns

Best fit means ______________________________

1. ______________________________

____

2. ____________________

Hiding cells is ____________________

3. ____________________

4. ____________________

5. ____________________

☞ To change the height of rows

1. ____________________

2. ____________________

3. ____________________

VIII. Checking spelling [EX 112]

Use Excel's spell checker to check ____________________

☞ To check spelling on the worksheet

1. ____________________

2. ____

____

3. ____

____

____

A. Additional spelling checker considerations [EX 113]

Consider these additional guidelines when using the spell checker:

1. ____
2. ____
3. ____
4. ____
5. ____
6. ____
7. ____

____

IX. Preparing to print the worksheet [EX 114]

Page Layout view allows you to ______________________________

The default view is ______________________________

A header is ______________________________

☞ To change the worksheet's margins, header, and orientation in Page Layout view

Margins are ______________________________

1. ____
2. ____

____

3. ____

____

____

____

4. ____
5. ____

X. Printing the worksheet [EX 117]

☞ To print a worksheet

1. ____
2. ____
3. ____

4. ______________________________

5. ______________________________

☞ To print a section of the worksheet

1. ______________________________

____

____

2. ______________________________

____

____

XI. Displaying and printing the formulas version of the worksheet [EX 119]

The values version shows ______________________________

The formulas version displays ______________________________

The formulas version of a worksheet is useful for debugging. Debugging is ______________

____

☞ To display the formulas in the worksheet and fit the printout on one page

1. ______________________________

____

2. ______________________________

3. ______________________________

____

4. ______________________________

____

5. ______________________________

____

Review

Matching (5)

If the value in cell B2 is 30, the value in cell B3 is 4, the value in cell C2 is 10, the value in cell C3 is 8, and the value in cell D2 is 2, match each formula on the left with its numerical equivalent on the right.

___	1. =B2 + B3 * C3 – C2 / D2	53
___	2. =C2 ^ 2 – B2 / D2 – B3 * C3	48
___	3. =D2 * C3 + B3 * B2 / C2	28
___	4. =B2 – B3 ^ 2 / C3 + C2 * D2	54
___	5. =C3 * C2 – B3 ^ D2 – B2	57
		62
		34

True-False (5)

*Circle **T** if the statement is true and **F** if the statement is false.*

T F 1. A function takes a value or values, performs an operation, and returns a value or values.

T F 2. The default row height in a blank worksheet is 8.43 characters (or 64 pixels).

T F 3. When the format you assign to a cell causes the entry to exceed the width of a column, Excel automatically changes the column width to best fit.

T F 4. If you decrease column width to zero, the column is hidden.

T F 5. To check the spelling of the text in a single cell, select the cell so that the formula bar is not active and then start the spelling checker.

Modified True-False (5)

*Circle **T** if the statement is true. If the statement is false, circle **F** and make the statement true by writing the replacement for the underlined word or phrase in the blank.*

T F 1. A(n) banner is common content that prints on every page of a worksheet.

____

T F 2. The results version of the worksheet shows the results of the formulas you have entered, rather than the formulas themselves.

____

T F 3. One of the reasons Excel is such a valuable tool is that you can assign a(n) function to a cell and Excel will calculate the result.

____

T F 4. Excel has a function called the TOP function that displays the highest value in a range.

____

T F 5. You can toggle between the values version and formulas version of a worksheet by pressing CTRL+ACCENT MARK (`) to the left of the number 1 key.

____

Definitions (5)

Briefly define each term.

1. margins ________________
2. arguments ________________
3. conditional formatting ________________
4. pixels ________________
5. best fit ________________

The Excel Screen (5)

Identify the elements indicated in Figure EX3.

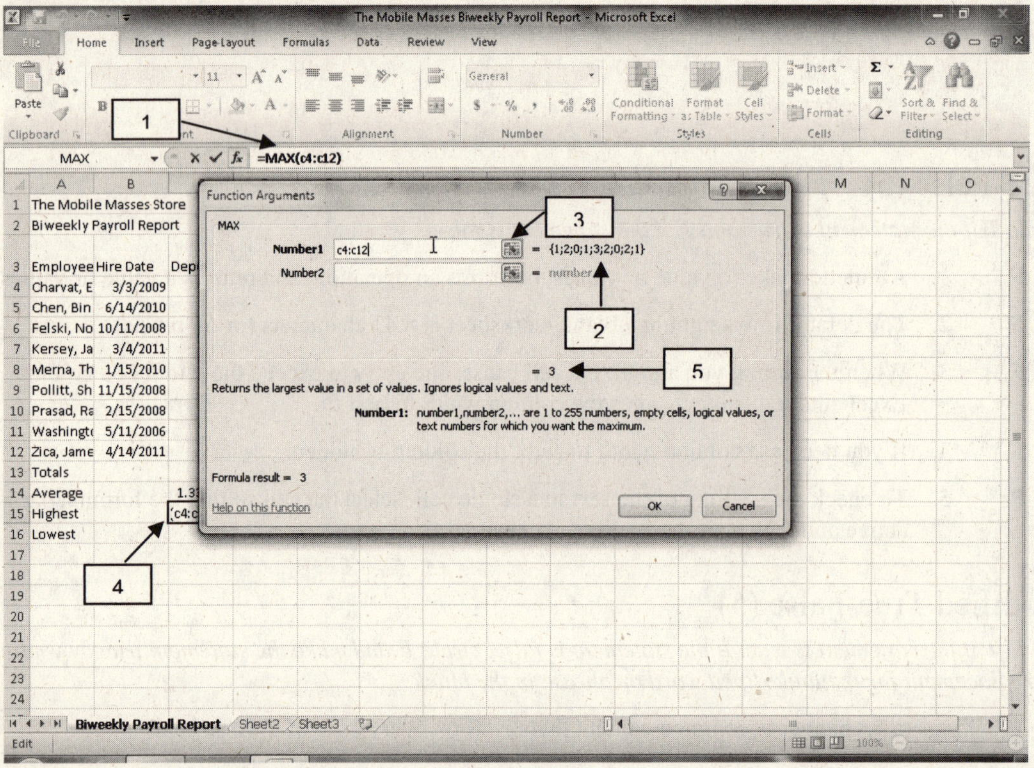

Figure EX3

1. ________________
2. ________________
3. ________________
4. ________________
5. ________________

Multiple Choice (5)

Circle the letter of the best answer.

1. Which of the following formulas would have the same numerical value as =C2 + D2 * E2 – F2?
   a. =(C2 + D2) * E2 – F2
   b. =C2 + D2 * (E2 – F2)
   c. =C2 + (D2 * E2) – F2
   d. =(C2 + D2) * (E2 – F2)

2. To determine the highest value in a range, what advantage does entering the MAX function have over simply scanning the range and entering the largest value as a constant?
   a. Excel recalculates the highest value each time you enter a new value in the range.
   b. It usually is easier to enter a function than to enter a number accurately.
   c. Excel does not change the result of a function, even if other values in a worksheet are altered.
   d. Functions can be entered using Point mode, but numbers can be entered only by using the keyboard.
3. Before adding a percent sign, how is the value displayed in a cell determined when the Percent Style button on the Ribbon is clicked?
   a. by adding 100 to the cell entry and rounding the result to the nearest percent
   b. by subtracting 100 from the cell entry and rounding the result to the nearest percent
   c. by multiplying the cell entry by 100 and rounding the result to the nearest percent
   d. by dividing the cell entry by 100 and rounding the result to the nearest percent
4. What is the name for a formula that contains a reference back to itself?
   a. self-reference
   b. circular reference
   c. auto-reference
   d. revolving reference
5. Which of the following comes first in the order of operations?
   a. percentages
   b. negation
   c. multiplication
   d. exponentiation

Dialog Box (5)

Answer the following questions about the New Formatting Rule dialog box shown in Figure EX4.

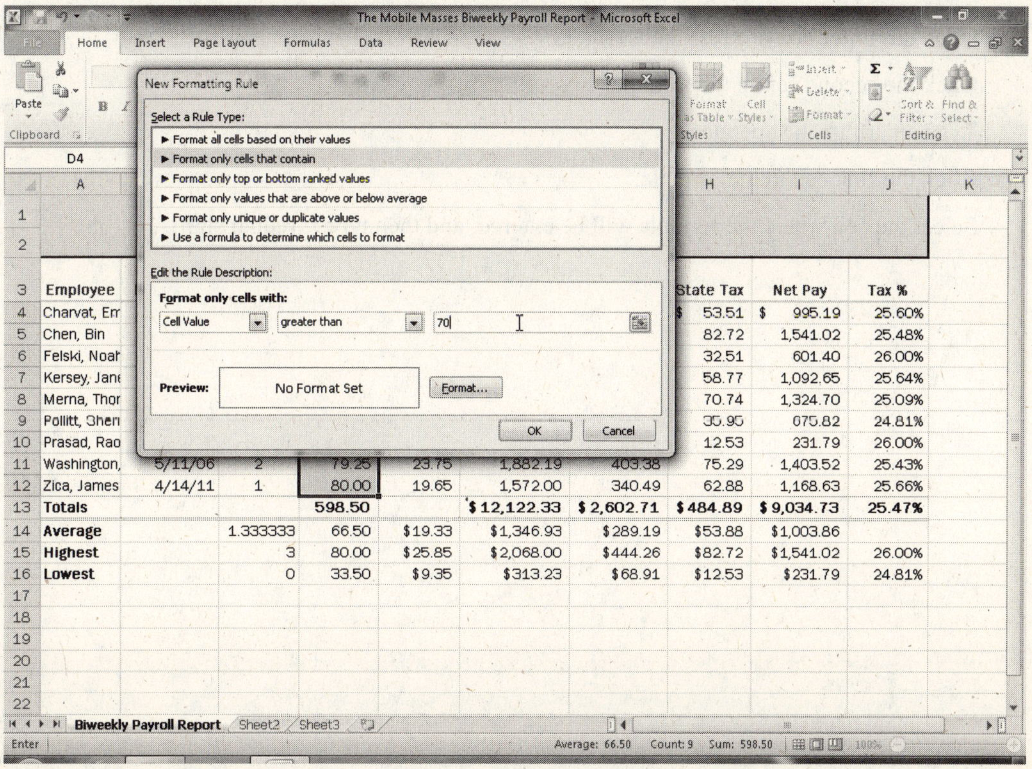

Figure EX4

1. How was the dialog box displayed? ______________________________
2. What does 'Edit the Rule Description' allow you to view? ______________________________
   ____
3. Which rule type is selected in this dialog box? ______________________________
4. Which button will open the Format Cells dialog box? ______________________________
5. What is value 70 in the dialog box? ______________________________

Fill in the Blanks (5)

Write a word (or words) in the blank to complete each sentence correctly.

1. A(n) ______________________ is a button that is automatically displayed on the screen, such as AutoFill options.
2. ______________________ is a technique you can use to hide data that might not be relevant to a particular report or sensitive data that you do not want others to see.
3. Formatting that appears only when values in the cell meet certain conditions is called ______________________ formatting.
4. ______________________ is the process of finding and correcting errors in a worksheet.
5. The ______________________ version of the worksheet shows the formulas you have entered, rather than the results of those formulas.

Sequence (5)

Use the numbers 1 – 5 to show the order in which these steps should be performed to enter a simple formula using Point mode.

___ Click the Enter box or press the ENTER key.

___ Click the second cell in the formula.

___ Type an arithmetic operator.

___ Click the first cell in the formula.

___ Select the cell where the formula will be entered, and then type = (equal sign).

Complete the Table

EXAMPLES OF EXCEL FORMULAS

Formula	Meaning
=K12	______________________
=10 + 4^2	______________________
______________________	Assigns three times the contents of cell C20 to the active cell.
=50% * 12	______________________
______________________	Assigns the negative value of the product of the values contained in cells H3 and Q30 to the active cell.
______________________	Assigns the product of 12 times the difference between the values contained in cells N8 and O8 to the active cell.
=M9 / Z8 – C3 * Q19 + A3 ^ B3	______________________ ______________________ ______________________ ______________________

Short Answer (5)

Write a brief answer to each question.

1. When should you use Point mode to enter formulas?

2. How do you select a range using the keyboard?

3. Why should you change the theme of a workbook?

4. What is the effect of applying the Accounting number format?

5. What happens if you change the column width to zero?

Activities

Expanding on Apply Your Knowledge

Perform the following tasks.

1. Open the Apply 2-1 Village of Scott Police Department in Apply Your Knowledge.
2. Change the workbook theme from Foundry to another theme using the Themes button (Page Layout tab | Themes group).
3. Change the font size, background color, and font color in cell A1.
4. Change the background color and font color in cell A2.
5. In cells C4:G4 and D13:G13, change the style to Comma style format with two decimal places.
6. In cells C5:G12, change the style to Accounting style format with two decimal places and fixed dollar signs.
7. In cells B4:B16, change the style to Accounting style with two floating dollar signs.
8. Use Range Finder to verify the formula in cell F13.
9. Save the revised announcement as Apply 2-1 Village of Scott Police Department_WKBK.

Expanding on the Lab

Perform the following tasks.

1. Open the Lab 2-1 Part 1 Aficionado Guitar Parts Accounts Receivable Balance Report workbook created in In the Lab 1.
2. Increase the beginning balance for each customer by $150.
3. Use Range Finder to verify the formula entered in cell G4.
4. Use conditional formatting to display bold white font on a blue background for any credits value greater than $75 in the range C4:C10.
5. Preview and then print the worksheet.
6. Display the formulas version of the worksheet. Print the formulas version of the worksheet in landscape orientation using the Fit to option on the Page tab in the Page Setup dialog box.
7. Save the workbook as Lab 2-1 Part 1 Aficionado Guitar Parts Accounts Receivable Balance Report _WKBK.

Microsoft Excel 2010

Chapter Three
What-If Analysis, Charting, and Working with Large Worksheets

Overview

In this chapter, you learn how to work with large worksheets that extend beyond the window and use the fill handle to create a series. The chapter also introduces new formatting techniques and the difference between absolute cell references and relative cell references. You also learn how to use the IF function, rotate text in a cell, freeze titles, add Sparkline charts, change the magnification of the worksheet, show different parts of the worksheet at the same time through multiple panes, create a 3-D Pie chart, and improve the appearance of a 3-D Pie chart. This chapter also introduces using Excel to do what-if analysis by changing values in cells and goal seeking.

Chapter Outline

I. Introduction [EX 138]

II. Project — Financial Projection Worksheet with What-If Analysis and Chart [EX 138]

  A. Overview [EX 141]

III. Rotating text and using the fill handle to create a series [EX 144]

  ☞ To rotate text and use the fill handle to create a series of month names

  1. ______________________________
     ____
     ____
  2. ______________________________
  3. ______________________________
     ____
  4. ______________________________
  5. ______________________________
     ____
  6. ______________________________
     ____

A. Using the AutoFill Options menu [EX 148]

☞ To increase column widths and enter row titles

1. ____

____

2. ____

____

____

3. ____

____

☞ To enter row titles

1. ____

____

____

2. ____

IV. Copying a range of cells to a nonadjacent destination area [EX 151]

☞ To copy a range of cells to a nonadjacent destination area

The Office Clipboard allows ______________________________

____

1. ____

____

2. ____

____

3. ____

A. Using the Paste Options menu [EX 152]

After the Paste button is clicked, Excel displays ______________

B. Using drag and drop to move or copy cells [EX 153]

The mouse pointer changes to a block arrow when ______________

Drag and drop is ______________________________________

C. Using cut and paste to move cells [EX 154]

Another way to move cells is to __________________________

____

V. Inserting and deleting cells in a worksheet [EX 154]

☞ To insert a row

1. ____

2. ______________________________

____

3. ______________________________

____

A. Inserting columns [EX 156]

To insert columns ______________________________

B. Inserting single cells or a range of cells [EX 156]

The Insert command on the shortcut menu or the Insert Cells command on the Insert list of the Insert button allows you to ______________________________

C. Deleting columns and rows [EX 156]

The error message #REF! indicates ______________________________

☞ To enter numbers with format symbols

Enter a number with a format symbol to display ______________________________

Valid format symbols include ______________________________

If the number entered with a format symbol

- is a whole number, it is displayed ______________________________
- has decimal places, it is displayed ______________________________

1. ______________________________

Freezing the titles is ______________________________

☞ To freeze column and row titles

1. ______________________________

____

____

2. ______________________________

☞ To enter and format the system date

A date stamp shows ______________________________

Use the NOW function to enter ______________________________

1. ______________________________

____

____

2. ______________________________

____

____

3. ______________________________

____

____

4. ______________________________

VI. Absolute versus relative addressing [EX 162]

An absolute cell reference instructs ______

A relative cell reference instructs ______

A mixed cell reference is ______

☞ To enter a formula containing absolute cell references

1. ______

2. ______

3. ______

VII. Making decisions — the IF function [EX 164]

The IF function is useful when ______

The general form of the IF function is ______

☞ To enter an IF function

1. ______

2. ______

☞ To copy formulas with absolute cell references using the fill handle

1. ______

2. ______

A. Nested forms of the IF function [EX 170]

A nested IF function is ______

VIII. Adding and formatting Sparkline charts [EX 170]

A Sparkline chart provides ______

☞ To add a Sparkline chart to a worksheet

1. ______

2. ______

3. ______

☞ To format and copy the Sparkline chart

1. ______________________________

2. ______________________________

IX. Formatting the worksheet [EX 173]

☞ To assign formats to nonadjacent ranges

1. ______________________________

2. ______________________________

3. ______________________________

☞ To format the worksheet titles

1. ______________________________

2. ______________________________

☞ To copy a cell's format using the Format Painter button

1. ______________________________

2. ______________________________

3. ______________________________

X. Adding a 3-D Pie chart to the workbook [EX 180]

A Pie chart is ______________________________

A chart sheet is ______________________________

Category names are ______________________________

The data series is ______________________________

An exploded Pie chart is ______________________________

☞ To draw a 3-D Pie chart on a separate chart sheet

1. ______________________________

2. ______________________________

3. ______________________________

☞ To insert a chart title and data labels

1. ______________________________

2. ______________________________

3. ______________________________

4. ______________________________

5. ______________________________

6. ______________________________

☞ To rotate the 3-D Pie chart

1. ______________________________

2. ______________________________

☞ To apply a 3-D format to the Pie chart

1. ______________________________

2. ______________________________

3. ______________________________

____

4. ______________________________

5. ______________________________

☞ To explode the 3-D Pie chart and change the color of a slice

Offsetting (or exploding) is ______________________________

1. ______________________________

____

2. ______________________________

____

3. ______________________________

____

____

XI. Renaming and reordering the sheets and coloring their tabs [EX 193]

☞ To rename the sheets and color their tabs

1. ______________________________

2. ______________________________

3. ______________________________

4. ______________________________

☞ To reorder the sheet tabs

1. ______________________________

XII. Changing the view of the worksheet [EX 196]

☞ To shrink and magnify the view of a worksheet or chart

1. ______________________________

____

2. ______________________________

3. ______________________________

☞ To split a window into panes

1. ______________________________

____

2. ______________________________

____

XIII. What-if analysis [EX 199]

What-if analysis (sensitivity analysis) is ______________________________

____

☞ To analyze data in a worksheet by changing values

1. ______________________________

☞ To goal seek

Goal seeking is used to determine ______________________________

1. ______________________________

2. ______________________________

3. ______________________________

4. ______________________________

A. Goal seeking [EX 202]

Goal seeking assumes ______________________________

Review

Matching (5)

Each formula on the left is copied from cell B5 to cell C6. Match each formula on the left with the formula from the right that would be entered in cell C6.

___ 1.	=B3 + B4	a.	=$B4 + C5
___ 2.	=$B$3 + $B$4	b.	=C4 + C$4
___ 3.	=$B$3 + B4	c.	=$B$3 + $B$4
___ 4.	=$B3 + B4	d.	=C4 + C5
___ 5.	=B3 + B$4	e.	=$C$4 + $C$5
		f.	=B$3 + C4
		g.	=$B$3 + C5

True-False (5)

*Circle **T** if the statement is true and **F** if the statement is false.*

T F 1. You can use the fill handle to create a series of numbers, dates, or month names.

T F 2. The general form of the IF function is: =IF(logical_test, value_if_false, value_if_true).

T F 3. If formulas reference cells in a deleted row or column, Excel adjusts these cell references.

T F 4. Window panes split by the vertical split bar scroll together vertically.

T F 5. Goal seeking assumes you can change the value of multiple cells referenced either directly or indirectly.

Modified True-False (5)

*Circle **T** if the statement is true. If the statement is <u>false</u>, circle **F** and make the statement true by writing the replacement for the underlined word or phrase in the blank.*

T F 1. Following the use of the fill handle, the <u>AutoFill Options</u> button remains active until you begin the next Excel operation.

____

T F 2. A versatile method of copying a source area is to use the Copy and Paste buttons on the <u>Insert</u> tab on the Ribbon.

____

T F 3. Valid <u>function</u> symbols include the dollar sign, comma, and percent sign.

____

T F 4. The <u>paste</u> operation is the only operation affected by an absolute cell reference.

____

T F 5. Use a(n) <u>bar</u> chart to show the relationship or proportion of parts to a whole.

____

Definitions (5)

Briefly define each term.

1. freezing titles ____

2. drag and drop ______________________________

3. date stamp ______________________________

4. what-if analysis ______________________________

5. Office Clipboard ______________________________

The Excel Window (5)

Identify the elements indicated in Figure EX5.

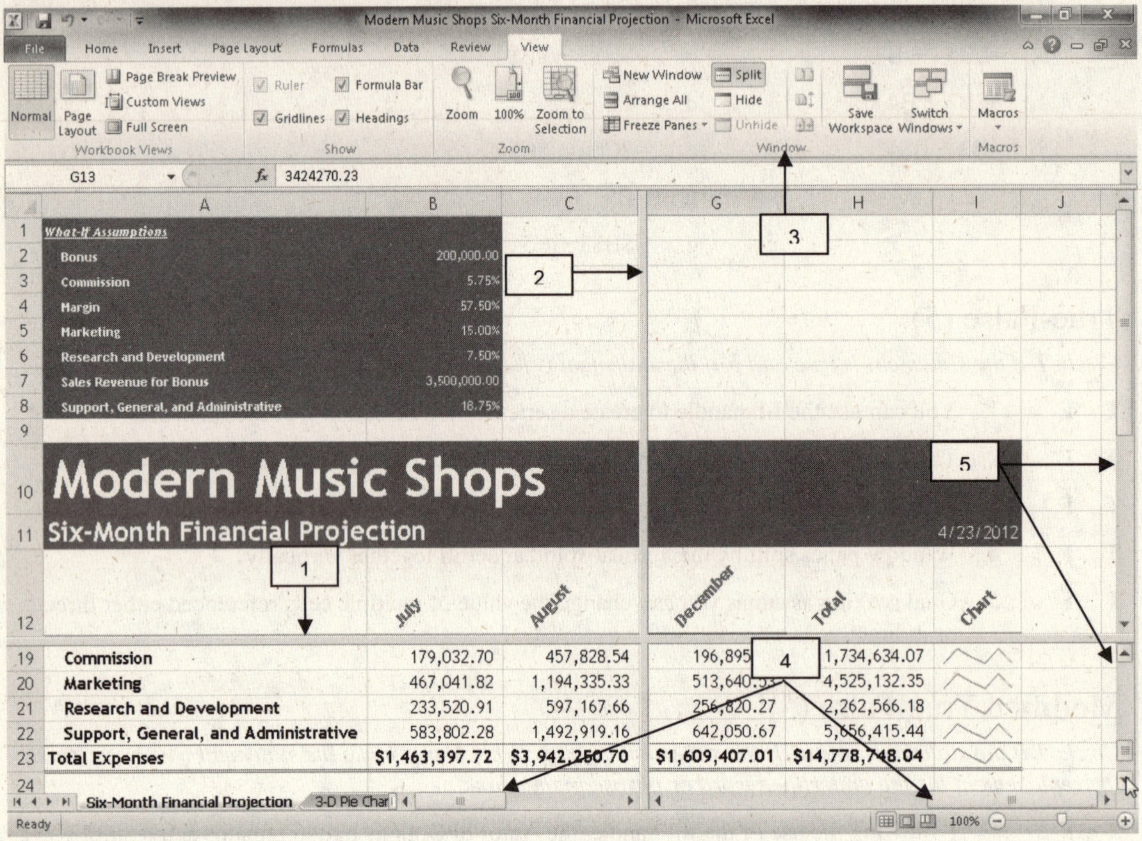

Figure EX5

1. ______________________

2. ______________________

3. ______________________

4. ______________________

5. ______________________

Multiple Choice (5)

Circle the letter of the best answer.

1. If $1234.5 is typed in the formula bar, what displays in the cell?
   a. $1234.5
   b. $1,234.5
   c. $1234.50
   d. $1,234.50

2. What function is used to enter the system date in a worksheet cell?
   a. DATE
   b. DAYS360
   c. NOW
   d. TIME

3. Cell B4 contains the value 100, and cell D5 contains the value 90. When the function =IF(B4 <> D5, 80, 70) is entered in cell E7, what value will display in cell E7?
   a. 100
   b. 90
   c. 80
   d. 70

4. In which of the following would both the column and row references remain the same when you copy the cell reference?
   a. B16
   b. $B16
   c. B$16
   d. $B$16

5. Which of the following is *not* a type of Sparkline chart?
   a. Column
   b. Pie
   c. Win/Loss
   d. Line

Dialog Box (5)

Answer the following questions about the Insert Function dialog box in Figure EX6.

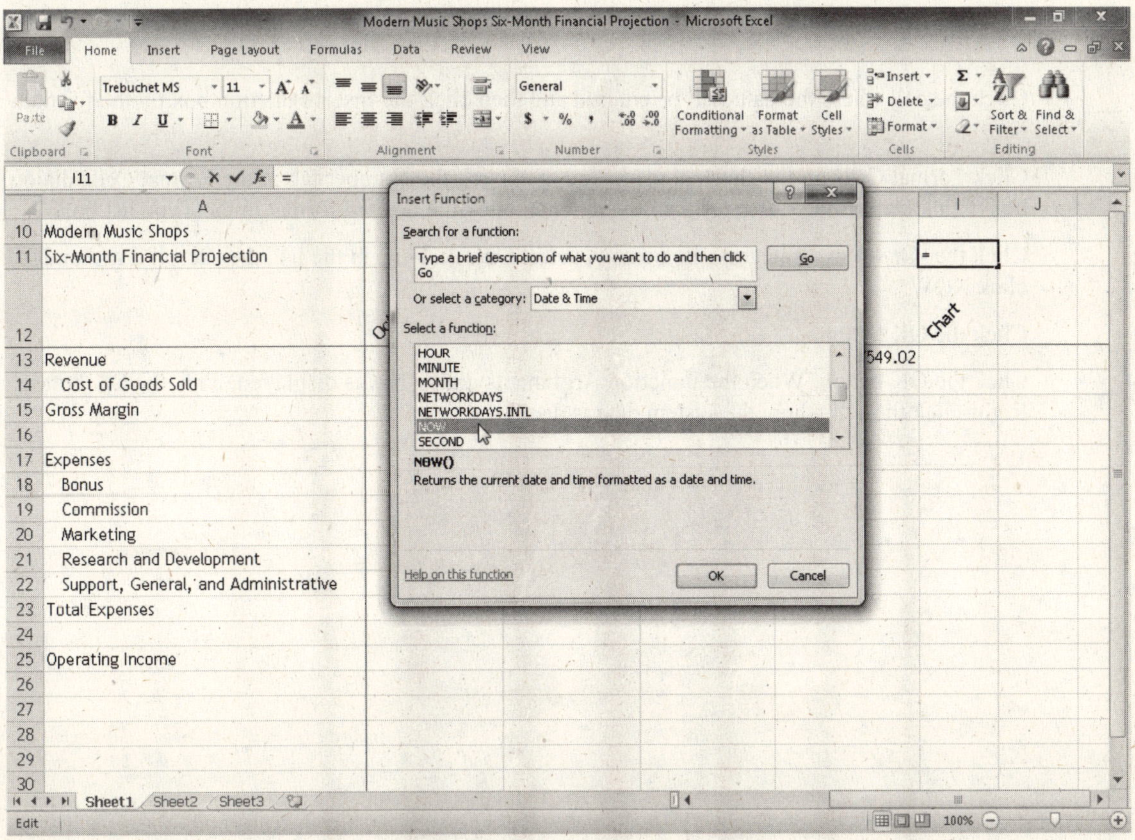

Figure EX6

1. How do you display the Insert Function dialog box? ______________________________
2. To what category does the selected function belong? ______________________________
3. What is the description of the selected function? ______________________________
   ____
4. What value will be displayed as a result of the selected function? ______________
5. How can you tell where Excel will place the inserted function? ______________

Fill in the Blanks (5)

Write a word (or words) in the blank to complete each sentence correctly.

1. A cell reference with only one dollar sign before either the column or the row is called a(n) ________________ cell reference.
2. The mouse pointer changes to a(n) ______________ when you are pointing to the border of a cell or range.
3. If cell A7 contains the formula =A4 + A5 and you delete row 5, then Excel displays the error message ______________ in cell A6 (originally cell A7).
4. Excel's ______________ function is useful when the value you want to assign to a cell is dependent on a logical test.
5. In accounting, negative numbers often are shown with ______________________ surrounding the value rather than with a negative sign preceding the value.

Sequence (5)

Use the numbers 1 – 5 to show the order in which these steps should be performed to enter and format the system date.

___ Click the cell where the date will be entered and then click the Insert Function box on the formula bar.

___ Click Format Cells on the shortcut menu and then click the Number tab in the Format Cells dialog box. Click Date in the Category list box and then click the desired format in the Type list box.

___ Click the -Or select a category- box arrow, select Date & Time in the list, then scroll down and click NOW.

___ Click the OK button.

___ Click the OK button. When the Function Arguments dialog box is displayed, click the OK button. Right-click the cell where the system date is displayed.

Complete the Table

EXAMPLES OF CELL REFERENCES

Cell Reference	Type of Reference	Meaning
\$B\$20	__________	____________________
B\$20	__________	____________________
\$B20	__________	____________________
B20	__________	____________________

Short Answer (5)

Write a brief answer to each question.

1. What is the function of rotated text in a cell?

2. What happens as you click the Increase X Rotation button in the Format Chart Area dialog box?

3. What is a good rule of thumb for offsetting slices of a Pie chart?

4. How do you make the decision regarding how tks and worksheets?

5. How does Excel format a date?

Activities

Expanding on Apply Your Knowledge

Determine the truth value (true or false) of the following logical tests, given the following cell values: X4 = 10; Y3 = 15; K7 = 220; Z2 = 9; and Q9 = 77. Enter true or false.

a. Y3 = 4 * (Q9 / 5) Truth value: ____________________

b. Q9 + K7 > 2 * (Q9 + 25) Truth value: ____________________

c. K7 + 300 <= X4 * Z2 + 10 Truth value: ____________________

d. Q9 * 2 – 42 < (X4 + Y3 – 8) / 9 Truth value: ____________________

e. K7 / Z2 > X4 – Y3 Truth value: ____________________

f. X4 + 15 * Z2 / 5 <> K7 Truth value: ____________________

g. Q9 = K7 Truth value: ____________________

h. Y3 < X4 Truth value: ____________________

Expanding on the Lab

Perform the following tasks.

1. Open the Lab 3-2 ReachOut Neighbor Analysis of Indirect Expenses workbook created in In the Lab 2.
2. Click the Indirect Expenses Analysis tab to display the worksheet.
3. A recently discovered leaky roof will require $5,000 worth of repairs to the Houston Branch Office. Increase the indirect expenses for Maintenance (cell D12) to $11,640.53.
4. Change the Chart Type to Doughnut. (*Hint*: Start by right-clicking the chart sheet.)
5. Print the revised worksheet and chart.
6. Because the Houston Branch Office must be closed for about five weeks while the leaky roof is repaired, ReachOut Neighbor will be satisfied if the Houston Branch Office's Net Income is $2,093.90 (90% of $2,326.55). Use the Goal Seek command to determine the Total Donations (cell D4) necessary to achieve the desired Net Income (cell D15) for the Houston Branch Office.
7. Print the resulting worksheet and chart.
8. Save the revised worksheet as Lab 3-2 ReachOut Neighbor Analysis of Indirect Expenses_WKBK.

Microsoft Access 2010

Chapter One
Databases and Database Objects: An Introduction

Overview

In this chapter, you learn to design a database, create an Access database, create tables and add records to them, print the contents of tables, create queries, create forms, and create reports. You also learn to change database properties.

Chapter Outline

I. Introduction [AC 2]

The term database describes ______________________________

____

Key features of a database management system include:

- ______________________
- ______________________
- ______________________
- ______________________
- ______________________

II. Project — Database Creation [AC 2]

In a relational database, a database consists of ______________________________

____

Records are ______________________________

A field contains ______________________________

A unique identifier, or primary key, is ______________________________

A. Overview [AC 4]

As you create a database, you should follow these general guidelines:

1. ______________________________
2. ______________________________
3. ______________________________
4. ______________________________
5. ______________________________
6. ______________________________

7. ______________________________

8. ______________________________

9. ______________________________

III. Designing a database [AC 6]

You can use a commonly accepted shorthand to represent the tables and fields that make up the database as well as the primary keys for the tables.

A. Database requirements [AC 6]

B. Naming tables and fields [AC 8]

The rules for table and field names are

1. ______________________________

2. ______________________________

3. ______________________________

4. ______________________________

C. Identifying the tables [AC 8]

Reasonable names for the tables in this chapter are Client and Business Analyst.

D. Determining the primary keys [AC 8]

Adding primary keys to the tables gives Client (Client Number) and Business Analyst (Business Analyst Number).

E. Determining additional fields [AC 8]

After identifying the primary keys, you need to determine and name the additional fields.

F. Determining and implementing relationships between the tables [AC 9]

The one-to-many relationship means ______________________________

____

____

G. Determining data types for the fields [AC 9]

Each field has a(n) ______________________________

The most commonly used data types are

1. Text – ______________________________

2. Number – ______________________________

3. Currency – ______________________________

H. Identifying and removing redundancy [AC 10]

Redundancy causes several problems, including:

1. ______________________________

2. ______________________________

3. ______________________________

☞ To start Access

1. ______________________________

____

____

2. ______________________________

____

IV. Creating a new database [AC 13]

You can create a new database in one of two ways: ______________________________

____

☞ To create a database

1. ______________________________
2. ______________________________
3. ______________________________
4. ______________________________
5. ______________________________
6. ______________________________

☞ To create a database using a template

1. ______________________________
2. ______________________________
3. ______________________________
4. ______________________________
5. ______________________________
6. ______________________________

V. The Access window [AC 15]

The Access window consists of a variety of components to make your work more efficient and documents more professional. These include ______________________________

____

A. Navigation Pane and Access work area [AC 15]

In the Access work area, you work on ______________________________

____

Object tabs appear ______________________________

The Navigation Pane contains ______________________________

____

The status bar presents ______________________________

____

VI. Creating a table [AC 15]

In Datasheet view, the table data is presented in ______________________________

Design view is used only to ______________________________

☞ To modify the primary key

1. ______________________________
2. ______________________________
____
____
3. ______________________________
____
4. ______________________________
5. ______________________________
____
____
6. ______________________________

☞ To define the remaining fields in a table

1. ______________________________
2. ______________________________
____
____
3 ______________________________
____

A. Making changes to the structure [AC 20]

- To undo your most recent change, click ______________________________
____
- To delete a field ______________________________
____
- To change the name of a field ______________________________
____
- To insert a field as the last field ______________________________
____
- To insert a field between existing fields ______________________________
____
- To move a field ______________________________
____

To start over, click ______________________________

☞ To save a table

1. ______________________________

2. ______________________________

____

☞ To view the table in Design view

1. ______________________________

2. ______________________________

B. Checking the structure in Design view [AC 22]

The row selector is used to ______________________________

____

☞ To close the table

1. ______________________________

☞ To add records to a table

A datasheet is ______________________________

1. ______________________________

2. ______________________________

____

3. ______________________________

4. ______________________________

____

____

5. ______________________________

____

6. ______________________________

____

C. Making changes to the data [AC 25]

- To undo your most recent change, click ______________________________

  ____

- To add a record, click ______________________________

  ____

- To delete a record, click ______________________________

  ____

- To change the contents of one or more fields in a record ______________________________

  ____

D. Starting Access and opening a database [AC 27]

☞ To open a database from Access

1. ____________________
2. ____________________
3. ____________________
4. ____________________
5. ____________________
6. ____________________
____

☞ To add additional records to a table

You use the Navigation buttons to ____________________
____

1. ____________________
2. ____________________
____
____
3. ____________________
4. ____________________

☞ To resize columns in a data sheet

Resizing means ____________________

Changing a column width changes the ____________________

1. ____________________
2. ____________________
____
3. ____________________
____

A hard copy or printout is ____________________

Green computing involves ____________________

VII. Previewing and printing the contents of a table [AC 30]

Portrait orientation means ____________________

Landscape orientation means ____________________

☞ To preview and print the contents of a table

1. ____________________
____

2.

3.

4.

VIII. Creating additional tables [AC 32]

A database typically consists of more than one table.

☞ To create a table in Design view

1.

2.

3.

4.

5.

6.

7.

8.

9.

10.

11. ______________________________

A. Correcting errors in the structure [AC 37]

You can use the following techniques to make changes to the structure:

- If you accidentally add an extra field to the structure ______________________________
- If you forget to include a field ______________________________
- If you made the wrong field a primary key field ______________________________
- To move a field ______________________________

IX. Importing data from other applications to Access [AC 38]

To import data means ______________________________

☞ To import an Excel worksheet

1. ______________________________
2. ______________________________
3. ______________________________
4. ______________________________
5. ______________________________
6. ______________________________
7. ______________________________
8. ______________________________

X. Additional database objects [AC 42]

☞ To use the Simple Query Wizard to create a query

Queries are ______________________________

1. ______________________________
2. ______________________________

3. ______________________________

____

____

____

4. ______________________________

____

5. ______________________________

____

6. ______________________________

7. ______________________________

8. ______________________________

A. Using queries [AC 45]

Queries are available for use in a variety of ways:

- ______________________________
- ______________________________
- ______________________________
- ______________________________

B. Creating and using forms [AC 48]

In Form view, you usually can see ______________________________

____

☞ To create a form

A form is ______________________________

1. ______________________________

____

2. ______________________________

3. ______________________________

____

4. ______________________________

C. Using a form [AC 50]

After you have saved a form, you can use it at any time by right-clicking the form in the Navigation Pane and then clicking Open in the shortcut menu.

D. Creating and printing reports [AC 51]

☞ To create a report

1. ______________________________

____

2. ______________________________

3. ______________________________

4. ______________________________

E. Using Layout view in a report [AC 53]

☞ To modify column headings and resize columns

1. ______________________________

2. ______________________________

3. ______________________________

4. ______________________________

5. ______________________________

6. ______________________________

☞ To add totals to a report

1. ______________________________

2. ______________________________

3. ______________________________

XI. Changing document properties [AC 58]

Document properties (metadata) are ______________________________

Keywords are ______________________________

Standard properties are ______________________________

Automatically updated properties include ____________________

____

☞ To change document properties

The Database Properties dialog box contains ____________________

1. ____________________

____

2. ____________________

3. ____________________

____

____

4. ____________________

XII. Special database operations [AC 60]

A. Backup and recovery [AC 60]

To recover a database means ____________________

A backup (or save) copy is ____________________

Backing up a database produces ____________________

The live database is ____________________

☞ To back up a database

1. ____________________

2. ____________________

3. ____________________

4. ____________________

5. ____________________

B. Compacting and repairing a database [AC 61]

When you compact a database, you ____________________

☞ To compact and repair a database

1. ____________________

2. ____________________

3. ____________________

C. Additional operations [AC 62]

☞ To open another database

1. ____________________

2. ____________________

3. ____________________

4. ____________________

☞ To close a database without exiting Access

1. ______________________________
2. ______________________________

☞ To save a database with another name

1. ______________________________
2. ______________________________
3. ______________________________
4. ______________________________

☞ To delete a table or other object in the database

1. ______________________________
2. ______________________________
3. ______________________________

☞ To rename an object in the database

1. ______________________________
2. ______________________________
3. ______________________________

Review

Matching (5)

Match each term on the left with the best description from the right.

___ 1. OLE object
___ 2. Yes/No
___ 3. Memo
___ 4. Calculated
___ 5. Attachment

a. the value of this kind of field is not actually stored
b. data type that can contain a chart, for example
c. data type that can be used as a hyperlink address
d. field that can store only one of two values
e. Access will increment the number in this kind of field by 1 as each new record is added
f. field that can store dates and times
g. field that can store a variable amount of text or combinations of text and numbers where the total number of characters may exceed 255

True-False (5)

*Circle **T** if the statement is true and **F** if the statement is false.*

T F 1. Redundancy usually results from placing too many fields in a table.

T F 2. To view the results of a query, open it by clicking it in the Navigation Pane and clicking View on the shortcut menu.

T F 3. The row selector is a small box or bar that, when clicked, selects the entire row.

T F 4. Report view is usually the easiest way to make changes to a report.

T F 5. By default, Access 2010 displays database objects in overlapping windows instead of as tabbed documents.

Modified True-False (5)

*Circle **T** if the statement is true. If the statement is <u>false</u>, circle **F** and make the statement true by writing the replacement for the underlined word or phrase in the blank.*

T F 1. <u>Green</u> computing involves reducing the environmental waste generated when using a computer.

____

T F 2. A field with the <u>Currency</u> data type can contain only monetary data.

____

T F 3. <u>Forms</u> are most commonly used for printing data.

____

T F 4. Names can be up to <u>32</u> characters in length.

____

T F 5. <u>Portrait</u> orientation means the printout is across the height of the page.

____

Definitions (5)

Briefly define each term.

1. task pane ____________________
2. Enhanced ScreenTip ____________________
3. layout ____________________
4. import ____________________
5. datasheet ____________________

The Access Window (5)

Identify the elements indicated in Figure AC1.

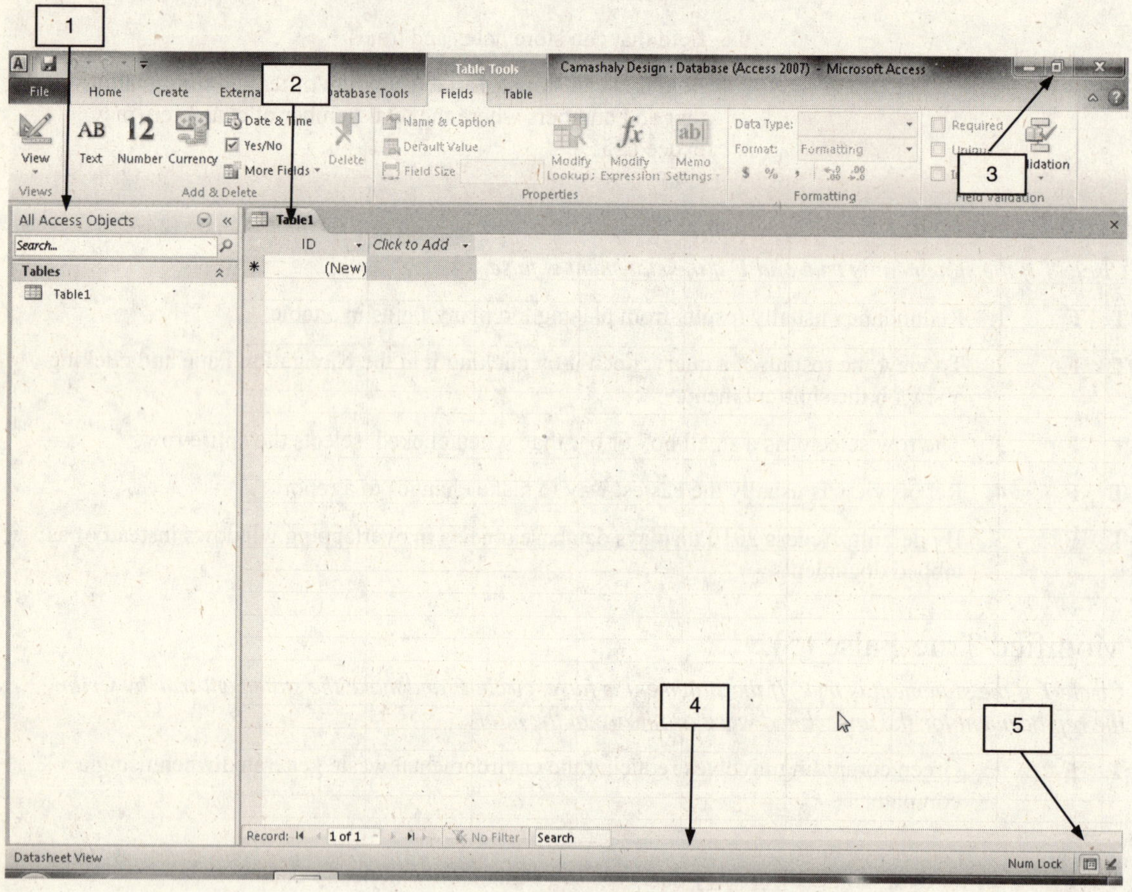

Figure AC1

1. ____________________ 4. ____________________
2. ____________________ 5. ____________________
3. ____________________

Multiple Choice (5)

Circle the letter of the best answer.

1. Which of the following is a character that can be used in a file name?
   a. *
   b. :
   c. |
   d. +

2. What is the small box that, when clicked, selects an entire row?
   a. row highlighter
   b. record identifier
   c. record highlighter
   d. row selector

3. Which of the following presents information about the database object?
   a. Navigation Pane
   b. object tab
   c. status bar
   d. Ribbon

4. What Number field size is appropriate for integer values in the range of 0 to 255?
   a. Byte
   b. Integer
   c. Long Integer
   d. Single

5. Which of the following includes such information as the file's author, title, or subject?
   a. formsheet
   b. query
   c. metadata
   d. split form

Dialog Box (5)

Answer the following questions about the Properties dialog box shown in Figure AC2.

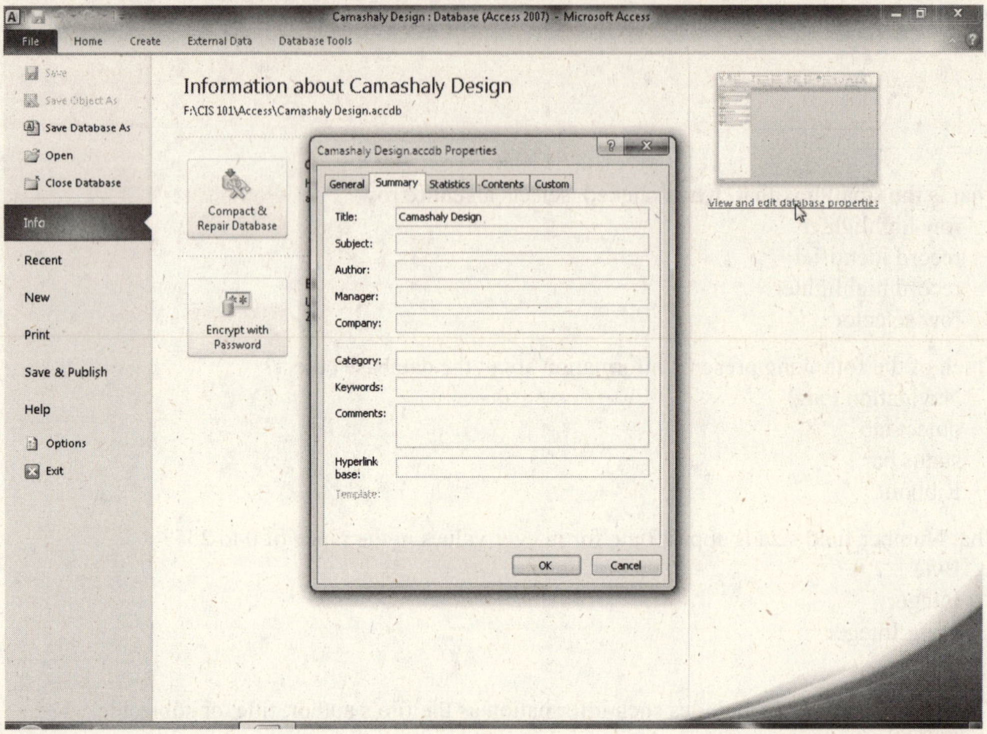

Figure AC2

1. How was the dialog box displayed? ____
2. Why would some of the database properties already be filled in? ____________________
____
3. What types of properties does Access collect automatically? ________________________
____
4. What is the function of the keywords? ____
5. What does the dialog box contain? ____

Fill in the Blanks (5)

Write a word (or words) in the blank to complete each sentence correctly.

1. If a problem occurs as you back up a database, you correct the problem by copying this backup copy over the actual database, often referred to as the ______________________ database.
2. The columns in a table are called ______________________.
3. To place the insertion point after the last data record before you can enter additional data, use the ______________________ buttons near the lower-left corner to move within the table.
4. If you discover a mistake before pressing the TAB key to move to the next field, you can correct it by first pressing the ______________________ key(s) and then typing the correct characters.
5. ______________________ are simply questions, the answers to which are in the database.

Sequence (5)

Use the numbers 1 – 5 to show the order in which these steps should be performed to use a criterion in a query.

___ Click the Close button for the query.

___ Click Design View on the shortcut menu to open the query in Design view.

___ Right-click the query in the Navigation Pane.

___ Click the View button to display the query results in Datasheet view.

___ Click the Criteria row in the column of the grid and then type the desired criterion.

Complete the Table

ADDITIONAL DATA TYPES

Data Type	Description
____________	Field can store a variable amount of text or combinations of text and numbers where the total number of characters may exceed 255.
Date and Time	____________
____________	Field can store a unique sequential number that Access assigns to a record. Access will increment the number by 1 as each new record is added.
____________	Field can store only one of two values.
OLE Object	____________
Hyperlink	____________
Attachment	____________

Short Answer (5)

Write a brief answer to each question.

1. What characters can you use in a file name?

2. What are the steps to compact and repair a database?

3. If you accidentally add an extra field to the structure, how do you remove it?

4. How do you change the contents of one or more fields in a record?

5. How can you recognize Layout view?

Activities

Expanding on Apply Your Knowledge

Perform the following tasks.

1. Open the Babbage CPA Firm database modified in Apply Your Knowledge.
2. Create a simple form for the Client table.
3. Open the form and bring the record with Client Number J77 to the screen.
4. Change the Balance Due for J77 (Jones Plumbing) to $125.00. Change the Bookkeeper Number to 34.
5. Switch to Datasheet view.
6. Print the table.
7. Change the Balance Due for J77 back to $0.00. Change the Bookkeeper Number back to 22.
8. Close the table.
9. Click No when asked if you want to save the form.
10. Create a report for the Client table using Module style.

Expanding on the Lab

Perform the following tasks.

1. Open the ECO Clothesline database created in In the Lab 1.
2. Open the Sales Rep table in Design view and change the field size for the Comm Rate field to Double.
3. Create a query using the Simple Query Wizard for the Sales Rep table that displays the Sales Rep Number, Last Name, First Name, State, Base Pay YTD, and Comm Rate fields. Use the name Sales Rep Query.
4. Create and save a report for the Sales Rep table that includes Sales Rep Number, Last Name, First Name, and Base Pay YTD fields. Include a total for the Base Pay YTD field.
5. Open the Sales Rep Query and add a criterion to limit retrieval to sales reps from North Carolina (NC). Save the query as Sales Rep-NC Query.
6. Create a simple form for the Sales Rep table.
7. Open the form and bring the record with Sales Rep Number 51 to the screen.
8. Change the First Name for 51 to Gabriel.
9. Close the table.
10. Click No when asked if you want to save the form.

Microsoft Access 2010

Chapter Two
Querying a Database

Overview

In this chapter, you learn to create queries, enter fields, enter criteria, use text and numeric data in queries, use wildcards, use compound criteria, create parameter queries, sort data in queries, join tables in queries, perform calculations in queries, and create crosstab queries. You also learn to create a report and a form that used a query, to export a query, and to customize the Navigation Pane.

Chapter Outline

I. Introduction [AC 74]

A database management system can answer questions. When you pose a question to a database management system such as Access, the question is called a query.

A query is ____

II. Project — Querying a Database [AC 74]

A. Overview [AC 76]

To design a query, you should follow these general guidelines:

1. ____

____

2. ____

____

3. ____

____

4. ____

____

5. ____

____

____

6. ____

____

____

☞ To start Access

1. ______________________________
2. ______________________________
3. ______________________________
4. ______________________________

☞ To open a database

1. ______________________________
2. ______________________________
3. ______________________________
4. ______________________________
5. ______________________________
6. ______________________________
7. ______________________________

III. Creating queries [AC 77]

Queries are simply ______________________________

☞ To create a query in Design view

1. ______________________________

____

____

2. ______________________________

____

____

____

☞ To add fields to the design grid

1. ______________________________

____

____

____

A. Determining criteria [AC 80]

☞ To use text data in a criterion

Text data is ______________________________

1. ______________________________

____

2. ______________________________

3. ______________________________

____

4. ______________________________

B. Using saved queries [AC 82]

After you have created and saved a query, you can use it in a variety of ways

- ______________________________
- ______________________________
- ______________________________
- ______________________________
- ______________________________
- ______________________________

____

☞ To use a wildcard

Wildcards are ______________________________

The asterisk (*) represents ______________________________

The question mark (?) represents ______________________________

1. ______________________________

____

____

____

2. ______________________________

____

3. ______________________________

4. ______________________________

____

5. ______________________________

☞ To use criteria for a field not included in the results

1. ______________________________

____

____

____

2. ______________________________

3. ______________________________

____

4. ______________________________

____

____

C. Creating a parameter query [AC 86]

A parameter query is ______________________________

☞ To create and view a parameter query

1. ______________________________

____

2. ______________________________

3. ______________________________

____

4. ______________________________

____

____

____

5. ______________________________

☞ To use a parameter query

1. ______________________________

____

____

2. ______________________________

____

☞ To use a number in a criterion

1. ______________________________

____

____

____

2. ______________________________

3. ______________________________

☞ To use a comparison operator in a criterion

Unless otherwise specified, Access assumes the criteria entered involve ______________

You must enter a comparison operator if you want ______________________________

Comparison operators:			
>	____________	>=	____________
<	____________	<=	____________
NOT	____________		

☞ To use a comparison operator in a criterion

1. ______________________________
____
____
2. ______________________________
3. ______________________________
____

D. Using compound criteria [AC 92]

A compound criterion is ______________________________

- An AND criterion is true provided ______________________________
____
- An OR criterion is true provided ______________________________

☞ To use a compound criterion involving AND

1. ______________________________
____
____
2. ______________________________
3. ______________________________

☞ To use a compound criterion involving OR

1. ______________________________
____
____
2. ______________________________
3. ______________________________

E. Special criteria [AC 94]

There are three special criteria you can use in queries:

1. You can use the AND operator if ______________________________
____
2. You can use the BETWEEN operator to ______________________________
____

3. You can use the IN operator to ______________________________

____

IV. Sorting [AC 94]

You sort records to order ______________________________

The sort key is ______________________________

- The major sort key (primary sort key) is ______________________________
- The minor sort key (secondary sort key) is ______________________________

The guidelines related to sorting in queries are

1. ______________________________

____

2. ______________________________

____

3. ______________________________

____

4. ______________________________

____

☞ To clear the design grid

1. ______________________________

____

____

2. ______________________________

☞ To sort data in a query

1. ______________________________

____

2. ______________________________

3. ______________________________

____

☞ To omit duplicates

A property sheet is ______________________________

1. ______________________________

____

____

____

2. ______________________________

3. ______________________________

4. ______

☞ To sort on multiple keys

1. ______

______

______

2. ______

______

3. ______

☞ To create a top-value query

A top-value query allows ______

1. ______

______

______

2. ______

______

3. ______

______

V. Joining tables [AC 100]

You join tables to find ______

The following are guidelines related to joining tables:

1. ______

______

2. ______

______

3. ______

______

4. ______

______

☞ To join tables

A join line is ______

1. ______

______

______

2. ______

______

______

3. ____

____

4. ____

5. ____

____

6. ____

☞ To change join properties

Join properties are ____

1. ____

____

2. ____

3. ____

____

____

4. ____

☞ To create a report involving a join

1. ____

____

____

2. ____

____

3. ____

____

____

4. ____

VI. Creating a form for a query [AC 108]

A form is ____

☞ To create a form for a query

1. ____

____

2. ____

3. ____

____

4. ____

____

A. Using a form [AC 110]

After you have saved a form, you can use it at any time by right-clicking the form in the Navigation Pane and then clicking Open on the shortcut menu.

VII. Exporting data from Access to other applications [AC 110]

To export means ____________________

☞ To export data to Excel

1. ____________________

2. ____________________

3. ____________________

4. ____________________

5. ____________________

☞ To export data to Word

1. ____________________

2. ____________________

3. ____________________

4. ____________________

A. Text files [AC 113]

In delimited files, each record is ____________________

A delimiter is ____________________

In fixed-width files, the width of any field is ____________________

☞ To export data to a text file

1. ____________________

2. ____________________

3. ____________________

4. ____________________

5. ____________________

6. ______________________________

7. ______________________________

VIII. Adding criteria to a join query [AC 114]

☞ To restrict the records in a join

1. ______________________________

2. ______________________________

3. ______________________________

IX. Calculations [AC 115]

A calculated (computed) field is ______________________________

A group calculation is ______________________________

The following are guidelines related to calculations in queries:

1. ______________________________

An alias is ______________________________

2. ______________________________

☞ To use a calculated field in a query

1. ______________________________

2. ______________________________

3. ______________________________

4. ______________________________

☞ To change a caption

1. ______________________________

2. ______________________________

3. ______________________________

☞ To calculate statistics

An aggregate function is ______________________________

1. ______________________________

2. ______________________________

3. ______________________________

4. ______________________________

☞ To use criteria in calculating statistics

1. ______________________________

2. ______________________________

3. ______________________________

4. ______________________________

☞ To use grouping

Grouping means ______________________________

1. ______________________________

2. ______________________________

3. ______________________________

X. Crosstab queries [AC 123]

A crosstab query calculates ______________________________

☞ To create a crosstab query

1. ____

   ____

2. ____

   ____

3. ____

   ____

4. ____

   ____

5. ____

   ____

   ____

6. ____

   ____

7. ____

   ____

☞ To customize the Navigation Pane

1. ____

   ____

2. ____

3. ____

   ____

4. ____

   ____

   ____

5. ____

Review

Matching (5)

Match each term on the left with the best description from the right.

___ 1. design grid
___ 2. text data
___ 3. comparison operator
___ 4. sort key
___ 5. join line

a. field on which the records are ordered in a particular way
b. drawn between matching fields indicating two tables are related
c. the area where you specify fields to be included in a query
d. symbol that indicates that all fields are to be included in a query
e. creating groups of records that share some characteristic
f. entries in a field whose type is any characters
g. used if you want something other than an exact match

True-False (5)

*Circle **T** if the statement is true and **F** if the statement is false.*

T F 1. If you wanted to sort the results of a query by city within state, city would be the major sort key and state would be the minor sort key.

T F 2. You are restricted to addition in calculations.

T F 3. In an OR criterion, each individual criterion must be true in order for the compound criterion to be true.

T F 4. To enter a number in a criterion, type the number without any dollar signs or commas.

T F 5. To clear the design grid, select all the entries and then press the DELETE key.

Modified True-False (5)

*Circle **T** if the statement is true. If the statement is false, circle **F** and make the statement true by writing the replacement for the underlined word or phrase in the blank.*

T F 1. A(n) calculated query calculates a statistic for data that is grouped by two different types of information.

____

T F 2. For group calculations, Access supports several built-in statistics, including SUM for calculating totals.

____

T F 3. The Access approach to queries is based on Query-By-Example.

____

T F 4. Any fields included in an expression must be enclosed in parentheses.

____

T F 5. The default join in Access is the outer join.

____

Definitions (5)

Briefly define each term.

1. query ______________________________
2. wildcards ______________________________
3. sort ______________________________
4. join ______________________________
5. grouping ______________________________

The Access Screen (5)

Identify the elements indicated in Figure AC3.

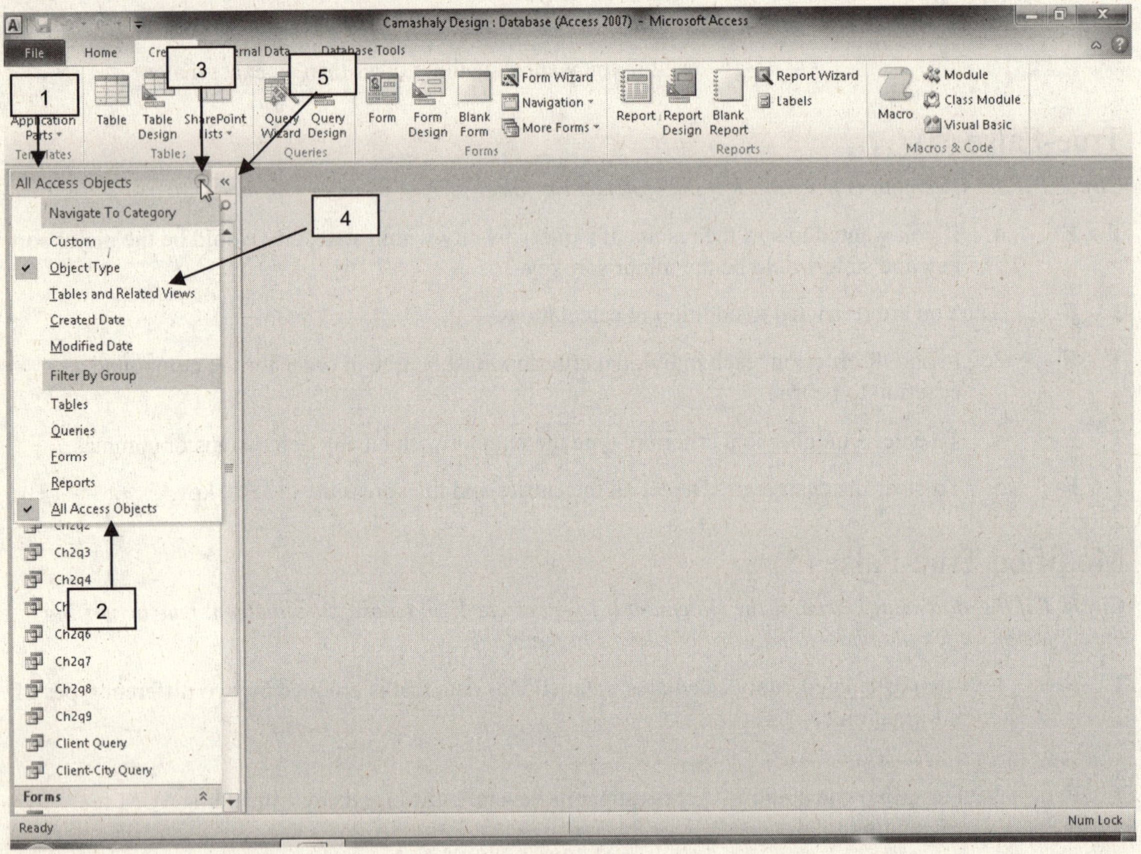

Figure AC3

1. ______________________________
2. ______________________________
3. ______________________________
4. ______________________________
5. ______________________________

Multiple Choice (5)

Circle the letter of the best answer.

1. How can you include all fields in a query without having to select each field individually?
   a. double-click the asterisk (*) in the field list
   b. leave the first column of the design grid blank
   c. type the word, ALL, in the first column of the design grid
   d. double-click the word, ALL, in the field list box
2. What wildcard represents any individual character?
   a. asterisk (*)
   b. exclamation point (!)
   c. ampersand (&)
   d. question mark (?)
3. Why would you place two criteria on the same line in the design grid?
   a. to specify sorting
   b. to specify an AND criterion
   c. to specify grouping
   d. to specify an OR criterion
4. What type of query allows you to quantify the results?
   a. append
   b. top-values
   c. quantification
   d. property
5. What statistic allows you to find the smallest value in a field?
   a. SMALL
   b. LOW
   c. MIN
   d. LEAST

Dialog Box (5)

Answer the following questions about the Show Table dialog box shown in Figure AC4.

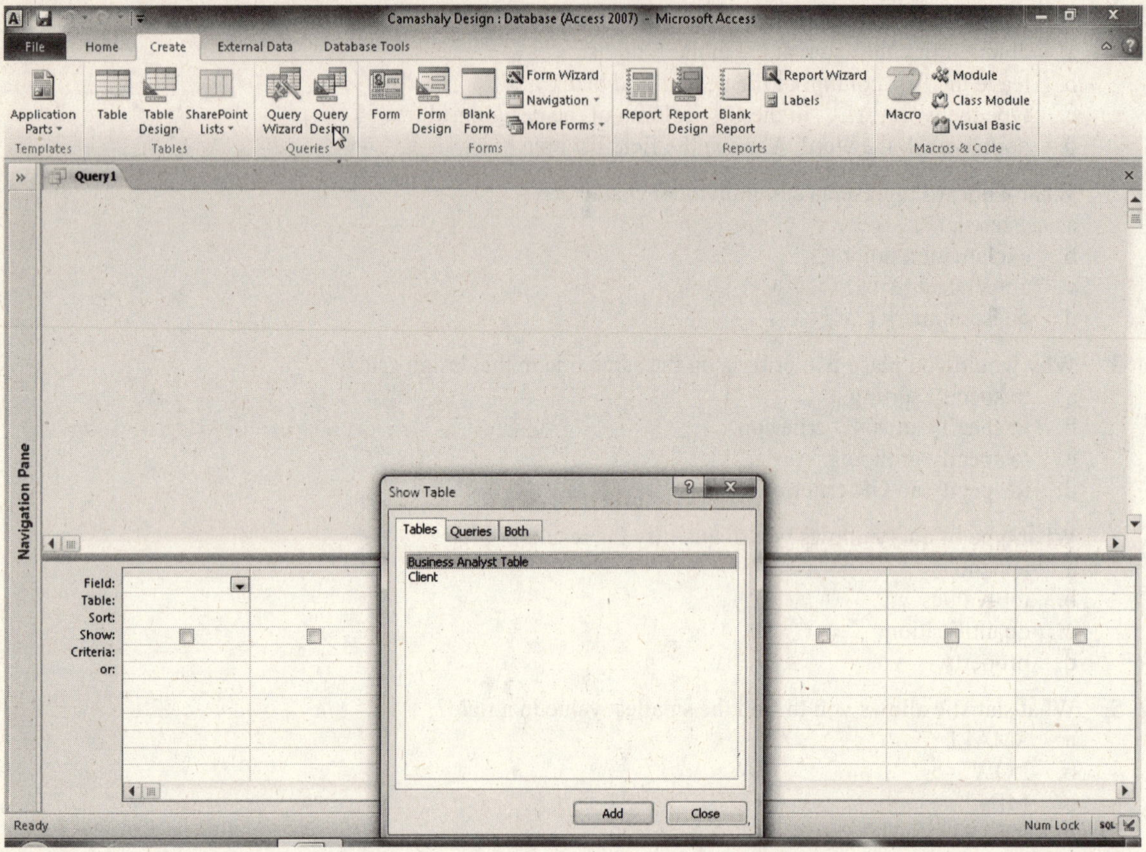

Figure AC4

1. How was the dialog box displayed? ______________________________
2. What tables are available to this query? ______________________________
3. How would you add the Business Analyst table to the query? ______________________________
4. How do you remove the dialog box from the screen? ______________________________
5. What table is currently selected? ______________________________

Fill in the Blanks (5)

Write a word (or words) in the blank to complete each sentence correctly.

1. A(n) ______________________ is a window containing the various properties of an object.
2. The ______________________ wildcard represents any collection of characters.
3. If you are sorting on more than one field, the more important field is called the ______________________.

4. A(n) ________________________ is a field that can be computed by performing operations (addition, subtraction, multiplication, or division) on other fields.

5. COUNT, SUM, and AVG are some of the built-in ________________________ that Microsoft Access supports.

Sequence (5)

Use the numbers 1 – 5 to show the order in which these steps should be performed to use criteria for a field not included in the results.

___ Type the criterion for the field not included in the results.

___ Click the View button to return to Design view, and erase any criteria.

___ View the query results.

___ In the design grid, include the fields in the query.

___ Click the Show check box to remove the check mark for the field not included in the results.

Complete the Table

COMPARISON OPERATORS

Operator	Description
>	________________________
<	________________________
>=	________________________
<=	________________________
NOT	________________________

Short Answer (5)

Write a brief answer to each question.

1. If you want to use a query in the future, do you need to save it?

2. If you are creating a query in Design view and you inadvertently add the wrong table, what should you do?

3. What is the purpose of the square brackets used in parameter queries?

4. Do you need to close a query before creating the next query?

5. If you are creating a join and you do not get a join line, what should you do?

Activities

Expanding on Apply Your Knowledge

Perform the following tasks.

1. Open the Babbage CPA Firm database modified in Apply Your Knowledge.
2. Use the Simple Query Wizard to create a query for the Bookkeeper table.
3. Include the Bookkeeper Number, First Name, and Last Name fields from the Bookkeeper table. Add a criterion for the Bookkeeper Number field that allows the user to enter a different Bookkeeper Number each time the query is run.
4. Assign the name, Bookkeeper Query_WKBK, to the query.
5. Create a query that joins the Bookkeeper table and the Client tables. Add the Client Number and Client Name fields from the Client table, and the Bookkeeper Last Name field from the Bookkeeper table. Sort the records in descending order by Client Number.
6. Save the query as Client-Bookkeeper Query_WKBK.
7. Use the Bookkeeper-Client Query already saved with the database to create a report like the one in Figure 2-89 on page AC 130, but remove the Client Number field from the report.
8. Save the report as Revised Bookkeeper-Client Report_WKBK and close the database.

Expanding on the Lab

Perform the following tasks.

1. Open the ECO Clothesline database modified in In the Lab 1.
2. Create a new query for the Customer table. Add the Customer Number, Customer Name, State, and Balance fields. Restrict retrieval to clients located in Virginia (VA) with a balance of $0.00.
3. Save the query as Lab 2-1 Step 2 Query_WKBK and print the results.
4. Create a query that includes the Sales Rep Number, Last Name, First Name, and State of all sales reps whose last names begin with G.
5. Save the query as Lab 2-1 Step 4 Query_WKBK and print the results.
6. Create a query to display the number of customers for sales rep 44.
7. Save the query as Lab 2-1 Step 6 Query_WKBK and print the results.
8. Create a query to display the average balance amount for customers from North Carolina (NC).
9. Save the query as Lab 2-1 Step 9 Query_WKBK and print the results.
10. Close the database.

Microsoft Access 2010

Chapter Three
Maintaining a Database

Overview

In this chapter, you learn how to use a form to add records to a table, search for records, delete records, and filter records, create and use lookup fields, create a calculated field, create and use multivalued fields, make mass changes, create validation rules, change the appearance of a datasheet, specify referential integrity, and use subdatasheets.

Chapter Outline

I. Introduction [AC 138]

Maintaining the database means ______________________________

Periodically, maintenance can involve the need to restructure the database; that is, ____________

____

II. Project — Maintaining a Database [AC 138]

A. Overview [AC 139]

Guidelines to follow for database maintenance

1. ____

____

____

2. ____

____

____

3. ____

____

____

4. ____

____

____

5. ____

____

6. ______________________________

III. Updating records [AC 141]

A. Adding records [AC 141]

A split form is ______________________________

☞ To create a split form

1. ______________________________

2. ______________________________

3. ______________________________

4. ______________________________

5. ______________________________

☞ To use a form to add records

1. ______________________________

2. ______________________________

☞ To search for a record

Searching means ______________________________

1. ______________________________

2. ______________________________

3. ______________________________

☞ To update the contents of a record

1. ______________________________

☞ To delete a record

To delete a record means to ____________________

1. ____________________

____

2. ____________________

3. ____________________

IV. Filtering records [AC 147]

A filter is used to ____________________

If you determine that only those records that satisfy some criterion should appear, you have two choices: ____________________

The following guidelines apply to this decision:

1. ____________________

2. ____________________

3. ____________________

If you have decided to use a filter, you need to decide which type of filter to use:

1. ____________________

2. ____________________

3. ____________________

4. ____________________

☞ To use Filter by Selection

1. ____________________

____

____

2. ____________________

3. ____________________

____

☞ To toggle a filter

1. ____________________

____

☞ To use a common filter

1. ____________________

____

2. ____________________

____

____

3. ____________________

4. ______________________________

☞ To use Filter by Form

1. ______________________________
2. ______________________________

☞ To use Advanced Filter/Sort

1. ______________________________
2. ______________________________
3. ______________________________

A. Filters and queries [AC 154]

Filters and queries are related in three ways:

1. ______________________________
2. ______________________________
3. ______________________________

V. Changing the database structure [AC 154]

A database's structure indicates ______________________________

The structure may have to be changed because ______________________________

☞ To delete a field

1. ______________________________
2. ______________________________
3. ______________________________
4. ______________________________

☞ To add a new field

1. ______________________________

____

____

2. ______________________________

____

☞ To create a lookup field

A lookup field allows the user to ______________________________

1. ______________________________

2. ______________________________

3. ______________________________

4. ______________________________

____

____

5. ______________________________

____

6. ______________________________

☞ To add a multivalued field

A multivalued field can ______________________________

The way to create a multivalued field is to ______________________________

____

☞ To add a calculated (compound) field

1. ______________________________

____

____

____

2. ______________________________

3. ______________________________

____

4. ______________________________

☞ To modify single or multivalued lookup fields

1. ______________________________

2. ______________________________

3. ______________________________

VI. Mass changes [AC 161]

Types of queries:

- Action query: ______
- Update query: ______
- Delete query: ______
- Append query: ______
- Make-table query: ______

☞ To use an update query

1. ______
______
2. ______
______
3. ______

☞ To use a delete query

Instead of deleting records individually, you can delete them in one operation using ______
______

1. ______
______
______
______
2. ______
______

☞ To use an append query

1. ______
2. ______
3. ______
4. ______
5. ______
______
6. ______

☞ To use a make-table query

1. ______
2. ______
3. ______
4. ______

5. ______________________________

____

6. ______________________________

An archive table is ______________________________

VII. Validation rules [AC 165]

Validation rules are ______________________________

Validation text is ______________________________

Validation rules can indicate a required field, establish a range of values, and specify a default value.

- A required field is ______________________________
- A range of values is ______________________________
- A default value is ______________________________

☞ To specify a required field

1. ______________________________

____

____

____

☞ To specify a range

1. ______________________________

____

____

☞ To specify a default value

1. ______________________________

____

☞ To specify a collection of legal values

A validation rule for a field can prevent Access from accepting any entry other than certain legal, or allowable, values.

1. ______________________________

____

____

☞ To specify a format

A format is used to ______________________________

A format symbol is ______________________________

____

- The format symbol > causes ______________________________

- The format symbol < causes ____________

1. ____________

☞ To save the validation rules, default values, and formats

1. ____________
2. ____________
3. ____________

A. Updating a table that contains validation rules [AC 169]

When updating a table that contains validation rules, Access

- Provides assistance in making ____________
- Helps in making ____________
- Will not accept ____________

If you cannot leave a field or close a table because you have violated a validation rule:

- Try again to type ____________
- Press the BACKSPACE key to erase ____________
- Use the ESC key until ____________

In drastic circumstances, correct the existing validation rules for the field.

☞ To change the contents of a field

1. ____________
2. ____________
3. ____________

☞ To use a Lookup field

1. ____________

☞ To use a multivalued lookup field

1. ____________
2. ____________
3. ____________

4.

☞ To update a form to reflect the changes in the table

1.

2.

3.

4.

5.

☞ To update a report to reflect the changes in the table

1.

2.

3.

4.

5.

☞ To include totals in a datasheet

1.

2. ____________

VIII. Changing the appearance of a datasheet [AC 179]

☞ To change gridlines in a datasheet

1. ____________

2. ____________

3. ____________

☞ To change the colors and font in a datasheet

1. ____________

2. ____________

3. ____________

A. Using the Datasheet Formatting dialog box [AC 182]

☞ To close the datasheet without saving the format changes

1. ____________

2. ____________

IX. Multivalued field in queries [AC 183]

☞ To query a multivalued field showing multiple values on a single row

1. ____________

2. ____________

☞ To query a multivalued field showing multiple values on multiple rows

1. ____________

2. ____________

3. ____________

X. Referential integrity [AC 185]

Referential integrity is ____________________

A foreign key is ____________________

A one-to-many relationship means ____________________

____

To cascade the delete means ____________________

To cascade the update means ____________________

☞ To specify referential integrity

1. ____________________
2. ____________________
3. ____________________

   ____

   ____
4. ____________________

   ____

   ____
5. ____________________
6. ____________________

   ____

A. Effect of referential integrity [AC 190]

☞ To use a subdatasheet

A subdatasheet displays ____________________

1. ____________________
2. ____________________

   ____
3. ____________________

B. Handling data inconsistency [AC 193]

☞ To find duplicate records

The Find Duplicates Query Wizard allows you to ____________________

1. ____________________
2. ____________________
3. ____________________
4. ____________________
5. ____________________

☞ To find unmatched records

The Find Unmatched Query Wizard allows you to ______________________

1. ______________________
2. ______________________
3. ______________________
4. ______________________
5. ______________________

XI. Ordering records [AC 193]

☞ To use the Ascending button to order records

1. ______________________

____

2. ______________________

____

____

____

☞ To use the Ascending button to order records on multiple fields

1. ______________________
2. ______________________
3. ______________________

Review

Matching (5)

Match each term on the left with the best description from the right.

___ 1. multivalued
___ 2. validation rule
___ 3. validation text
___ 4. required field
___ 5. default value

a. convention that the data entered by a user must follow
b. displayed in a particular field before the user adds a record
c. field in one table whose values are required to match the primary key of another table
d. field that can contain more than one value
e. message displayed if a user violates a validation rule
f. query that will delete all the records satisfying the criteria entered in the query
g. field in which the user actually must enter data

True-False (5)

*Circle **T** if the statement is true and **F** if the statement is false.*

T F 1. Updating can include mass updates or mass deletions.

T F 2. To reduce the size of a column, position the mouse pointer on the right boundary of the column's field selector and drag the line to the right.

T F 3. The property that requires the value in a foreign key to match another table's primary key is called entity integrity.

T F 4. To force all letters in a field to display as lowercase, use the asterisk (*) symbol in the Format property box.

T F 5. With a table that has validation rules, entering a number in a field that is out of the required range of the field will produce an error message in the form of a dialog box.

Modified True-False (5)

*Circle **T** if the statement is true. If the statement is <u>false</u>, circle **F** and make the statement true by writing the replacement for the underlined word or phrase in the blank.*

T F 1. You can add the results of a query to an existing table by using a(n) <u>additive</u> query.

____

T F 2. Before you change a(n) <u>data type</u>, you should consider what effect the change will have on other database objects.

____

T F 3. You <u>cannot</u> include wildcards in validation rules.

____

T F 4. Changing a column width changes the <u>layout</u> of a table.

____

T F 5. When entering data into a field with a validation rule, if you find that Access displays an error message and you are unable to make the necessary correction, you can press the <u>ALT</u> key until the record is removed from the screen.

____

Definitions (5)

Briefly define each term.

1. update query ______________________________
2. format symbol ______________________________
3. referential integrity ______________________________
4. foreign key ______________________________
5. subdatasheet ______________________________

The Access Screen (5)

Identify the elements indicated in Figure AC5.

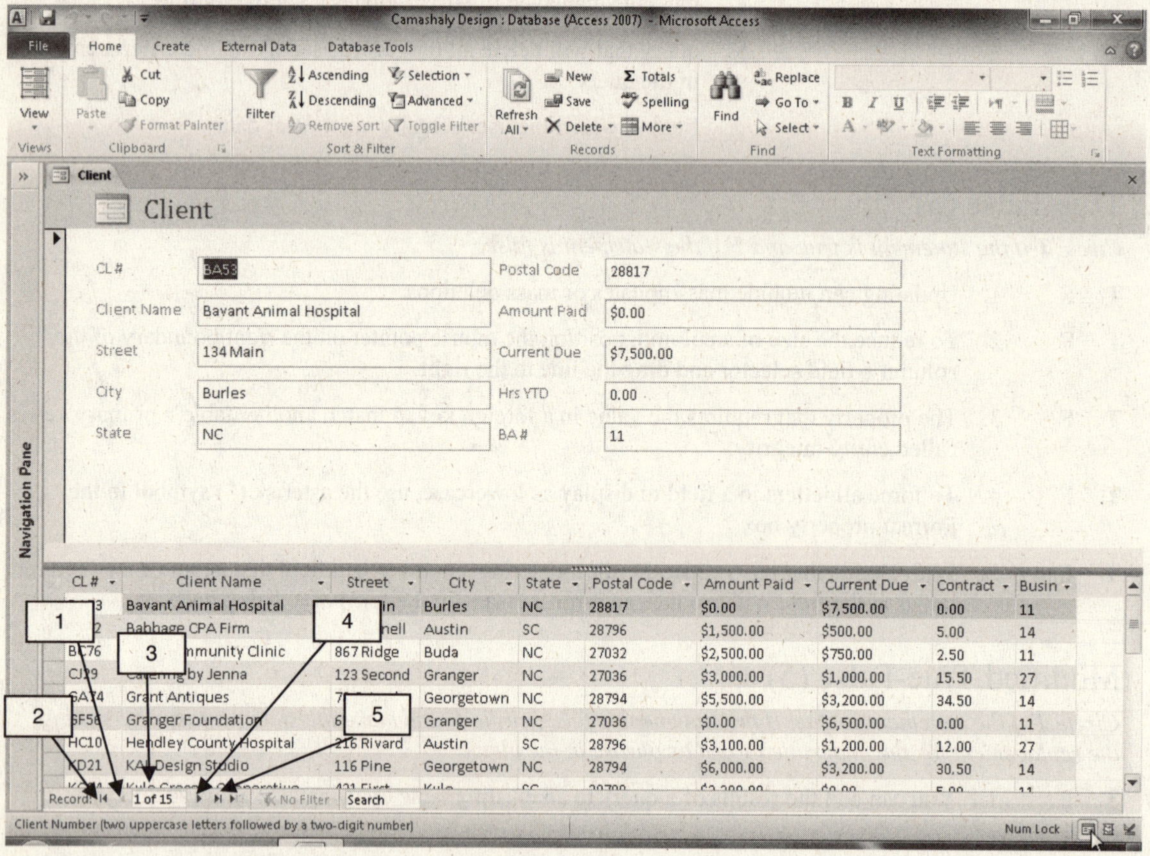

Figure AC5

1. ______________________________
2. ______________________________
3. ______________________________
4. ______________________________
5. ______________________________

Multiple Choice (5)

Circle the letter of the best answer.

1. Which kind of table contains data that is no longer used in operations but that might still be needed by the organization?
   a. historical
   b. compacted
   c. index
   d. archive

2. Which format symbol causes Access to convert uppercase letters automatically to lowercase?
   a. >
   b. /
   c. ~
   d. <

3. Which condition should be entered in the Validation Rule text box to ensure that entries in a currency field are between $0.00 and $500.00?
   a. >$0 and <$500
   b. >0 and <500
   c. >=$0.00 and <=$500.00
   d. >=0 and <=500

4. Which of the following terms refers to looking for records that satisfy some criteria?
   a. tracing
   b. sorting
   c. seeking
   d. searching

5. Which of the following is not a type of filter?
   a. Filter by Form
   b. Filter by Selection
   c. Common Filters
   d. Filter by Key

Dialog Box (5)

Answer the following questions about the Expression Builder dialog box shown in Figure AC6.

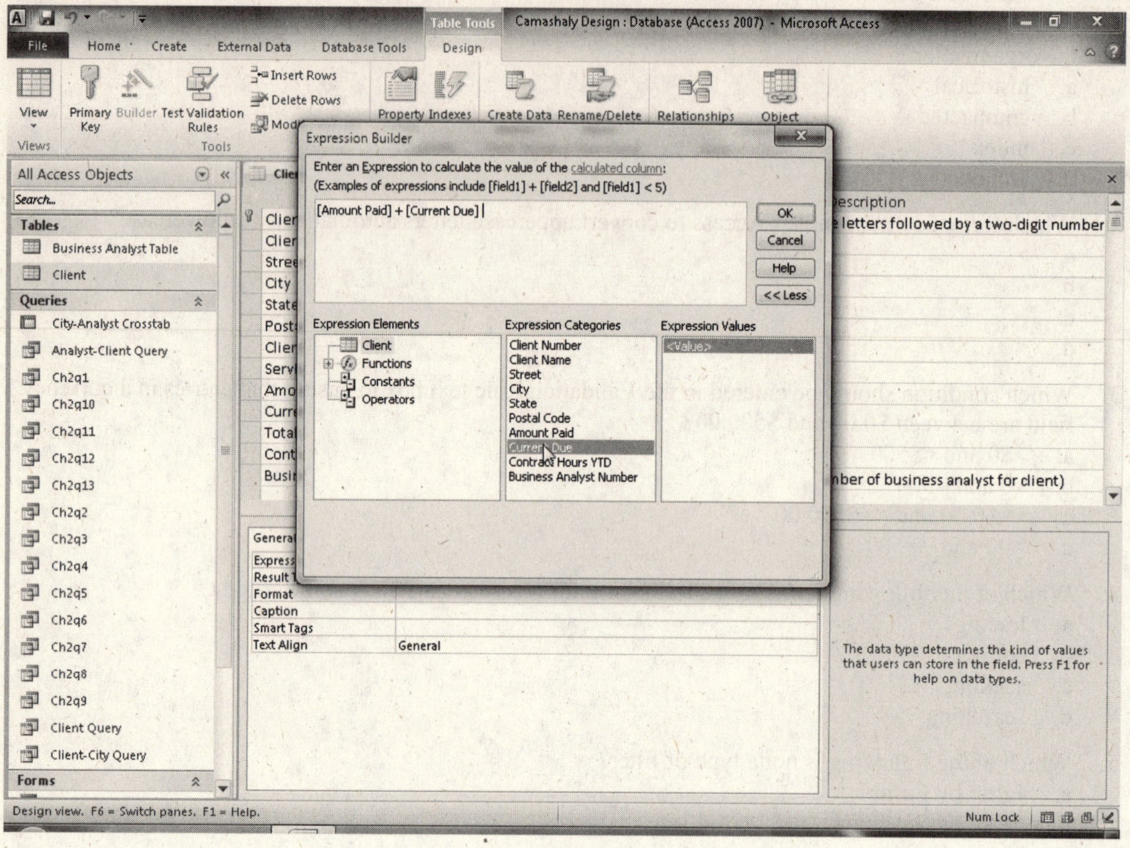

Figure AC6

1. How was the dialog box displayed? ______________________
2. Are users able to update the field being created in this dialog box? ______________________
3. How do you add a field to an expression? ______________________
4. What are the two ways of adding a plus sign to the expression? ______________________
____
5. Can you type the expression in the dialog box instead of selecting the fields from a list? ______________________
____

Fill in the Blanks (5)

Write a word (or words) in the blank to complete each sentence correctly.

1. Do not add a(n) ______________________ field to a table if you plan to also use the database with Access 2007.
2. When you create a database, you define its ______________________; that is, you indicate the names, types, and sizes of all fields.

3. You can use a(n) ______________________ to affect the way data is displayed in a field.

4. A(n) ______________________ rule is one that a user must follow when entering the data.

5. A(n) ______________________ field allows a user to select from a list of values.

Sequence (5)

Use the numbers 1 – 5 to show the order in which these steps should be performed to use a make-table query.

___ In Design view, indicate the fields to include, enter any necessary criteria, view the query results to be sure you have specified the correct data, and then return to Design view.

___ When Access indicates the number of records to be inserted, click the OK button.

___ Click the Make Table button.

___ Specify the name of the table to receive the new records and its location, and run the query.

___ Create a query for the table containing the records to add.

Complete the Table

MASS CHANGES

Query Type	Description
______________	Adds, deletes, or changes data in a table
Update query	______________________________ ______________________________
______________	Allows you to delete all the records satisfying some criterion
Append query	______________________________ ______________________________
______________	Allows you to add the results to a new table

Short Answer (5)

Write a brief answer to each question.

1. What are the three ways in which filters and queries are related?

2. If you are using Filter by Form, is there any difference in the process if you are viewing a table in Datasheet view rather than in Form view, or in a split form?

In your database, Employee Numbers are supposed to be four characters long. Is there a way for you to ensure that users do not type more than four characters?

4. How can you hide a subdatasheet when you no longer want it to appear?

5. If you plan to move your data to SQL Server at a later date, which kind of field should you not use, and why?

Activities

Expanding on Make It Right

Perform the following tasks.

1. Open the Senior Jobbers database modified in Make It Right.
2. Modify the multivalued Job Type field to include Replace Air Filters as a job type.
3. Change the referential integrity between the Worker and Customer tables so that you *will* cascade the update.
4. Use the Find Unmatched Query Wizard to find all records in the Worker table that do not match records in the Customer table. Worker Number is the common field in both tables. Include the Worker Number, Last Name, and First Name in the query. Name the query Worker Unmatched Query. Close the query.

Expanding on the Lab

Perform the following tasks.

1. Open the Walburg Energy Alternatives database from In the Lab 2. Open the Item table in Design view.
2. Add a Lookup field, Item Type, to the Item table. The field should appear after the Description field. The field will categorize the type of item. The types are ELEC (electronic device), MECH (mechanical device), and MISC (miscellaneous).
3. Make Item Type an optional field.
4. Change the number on hand to be between 5 and 80.
5. Save the changes to the table design. If a dialog box appears to indicate that some data may be lost, click the Yes button.
6. Using a query, assign the value MISC to the Item Type field for all records. Save the query as Update Query_WKBK.
7. Create an advanced filter for the Item table. The filter should display the item number, item type, description, and number on hand for all items with more than 15 items on hand. Sort the filter by item number. Save the filter settings as a query and name the filter Reorder Filter_WKBK.
8. Using a query, delete all records in the Item table where the description starts with the letter R. Save the query as Delete Query_WKBK.
9. Compact the database.

Microsoft Outlook 2010

Chapter One

Managing E-mail Messages with Outlook

Overview

This chapter illustrates using Outlook to read, open, print, reply to, forward, format, delete, save, and send e-mail messages. You view and save file attachments as well as attach a file to an e-mail message. You learn how to add a courtesy copy to an e-mail message and set the importance of e-mail messages. Finally, you create a folder in the Inbox and move an e-mail message to the new folder.

Chapter Outline

I. Introduction [OUT 2]

Electronic mail (e-mail) is ______________________________

An e-mail program is ______________________________

An Internet service provider (ISP) delivers ______________________________

____

An e-mail profile includes ______________________________

A personal folders file (.pst file) is ______________________________

II. Project — Composing and Sending E-mail Messages [OUT 3]

A. Overview [OUT 4]

As you read, respond to, and create an e-mail message, you should follow these general guidelines:

1. ______________________________
2. ______________________________
3. ______________________________
4. ______________________________
5. ______________________________

   ____
6. ______________________________

   An attachment is ______________________________
7. ______________________________

   A virus is ______________________________

An antivirus program is ______________________________

____

B. Outlook account settings [OUT 5]

An e-mail address identifies ______________________________

A user name is ______________________________

A domain name is ______________________________

A password is ______________________________

☞ To start Outlook

1. ______________________________
2. ______________________________
3. ______________________________
4. ______________________________
5. ______________________________

☞ To open an Outlook data file

1. ______________________________

____

____

____

The Navigation Pane is ______________________________

The Inbox is ______________________________

2. ______________________________

____

____

____

III. Composing and sending e-mail messages [OUT 8]

The message header routes ______________________________

The subject line states ______________________________

The message area consists of ______________________________

A greeting line sets ______________________________

The message text informs ______________________________

A closing signals ______________________________

A signature line identifies ______________________________

☞ To compose and send an e-mail message

1. ______________________________
2. ______________________________

____

____

____

____

3. ______________________________

____

____

4. ______________________________

____

____

____

☞ To send an e-mail message

1. ______________________________

A. How e-mail messages travel from sender to receiver [OUT 11]

The outgoing e-mail server examines ____________________

SMTP (Simple Mail Transfer Protocol) is ____________________

A router is ____________________

The incoming e-mail server stores ____________________

POP3, the latest version of Post Office Protocol (POP), is ____________________

____

B. Working with incoming messages [OUT 12]

The message pane lists ____________________

The message list is ____________________

A closed envelope icon signals ____________________

An open envelope icon signals ____________________

A hard copy (printout) is ____________________

Spam (junk e-mail) is ____________________

A hyperlink is ____________________

☞ To read an e-mail message in the Reading Pane

The Reading Pane appears ____________________

1. ______________________________

☞ To open an e-mail message in a window

1. ______________________________

☞ To close an e-mail message

1. ______________________________

2. ______________________________

☞ To print an e-mail message

A backup is ______________________

1. ______________________
2. ______________________

____

☞ To print multiple copies of an e-mail message

1. ______________________
2. ______________________
3. ______________________
4. ______________________

C. Responding to e-mail messages [OUT 17]

☞ To reply to an e-mail message

1. ______________________
2. ______________________

____

3. ______________________

____

____

____

____

____

4. ______________________

☞ To forward an e-mail message

1. ______________________
2. ______________________

____

3. ______________________

____

____

____

____

____

D. Message formats [OUT 21]

Formatting refers to ______

Outlook offers three message formats:

- HTML: ______
- Plain Text: ______
- Rich Text: ______

Microsoft Exchange is ______

☞ To change the message format and send the message

1. ______
2. ______

☞ To delete an e-mail message

1. ______
2. ______

E. Spelling and grammar check [OUT 24]

☞ To check the spelling of a correctly typed word

1. ______
2. ______
3. ______

☞ To check the spelling of misspelled text

1. ______
2. ______

F. Saving and closing an e-mail message [OUT 27]

☞ To save and close an e-mail message without sending it

1. ______
2. ______
3. ______

G. Opening and modifying a saved e-mail message [OUT 29]

☞ To open a saved e-mail message

1. ______

2. ______________________________

☞ To include a courtesy copy recipient in an e-mail message

1. ______________________________

AutoComplete is a feature that ______________________________

____

☞ To attach a file to an e-mail message

1. ______________________________

2. ______________________________

____

____

3. ______________________________

____

____

4. ______________________________

☞ To set message importance for a single e-mail message and send the message

An importance level indicates ______________________________

A message sent with high importance displays ______________________________

The low importance option displays ______________________________

1. ______________________________

H. File attachments [OUT 33]

The Attachment preview feature allows you to ______________________________

____

☞ To preview and save an attachment

1. ______________________________

____

2. ______________________________

3. ______________________________

____

____

____

____

____

4. ______________________________

IV. Using Outlook folders to organize the Inbox [OUT 35]

Folders are ______________________________

☞ To create a new folder in the Inbox folder

1. ______________________________

____

____

2. ______________________________

____

____

3. ______________________________

☞ To move an e-mail message to a folder

A source folder is ______________________________

A destination folder is ______________________________

1. ______________________________

____

____

2. ______________________________

____

☞ To quit Outlook

1. ______________________________

Review

Matching (5)

Match each term on the left with the best description from the right.

___ 1. signature line
___ 2. message text
___ 3. closing
___ 4. message area
___ 5. message header

a. routes the message to its recipients
b. states the reason for the message
c. where you type an e-mail message
d. sets the tone of the message
e. informs the recipient or summarizes or requests information
f. signals an end to the message
g. provides the name on one line, followed by other information listed on separate lines

True-False (5)

*Circle **T** if the statement is true and **F** if the statement is false.*

T F 1. A brief message is more likely to be read than lengthy text.

T F 2. If the e-mail program cannot contact the outgoing e-mail server when the message is to be sent, it is never delivered.

T F 3. Standard grammar rules do not apply to e-mail messages.

T F 4. The default importance level for all new messages is low importance.

T F 5. The previewers in Microsoft Office 2010 are designed to provide additional security against potentially harmful code.

Modified True-False (5)

*Circle **T** if the statement is true. If the statement is false, circle **F** and make the statement true by writing the replacement for the underlined word or phrase in the blank.*

T F 1. A(n) PST delivers Internet access to a geographical location, either regionally or nationally.

____

T F 2. A(n) router is a device that forwards data on a network.

____

T F 3. A(n) closed envelope icon indicates a previously read (opened) message.

____

T F 4. A(n) red wavy underline indicates the text may contain a contextual spelling error such as the misuse of homophones.

____

T F 5. A(n) message sent with high importance displays a red exclamation point in the message header.

____

Definitions (5)

Briefly define each term.

1. e-mail ______________________________
2. Attachment Preview ______________________________
3. e-mail profile ______________________________
4. spam ______________________________
5. backup ______________________________

The Outlook Window (5)

Identify the elements indicated in Figure OUT1.

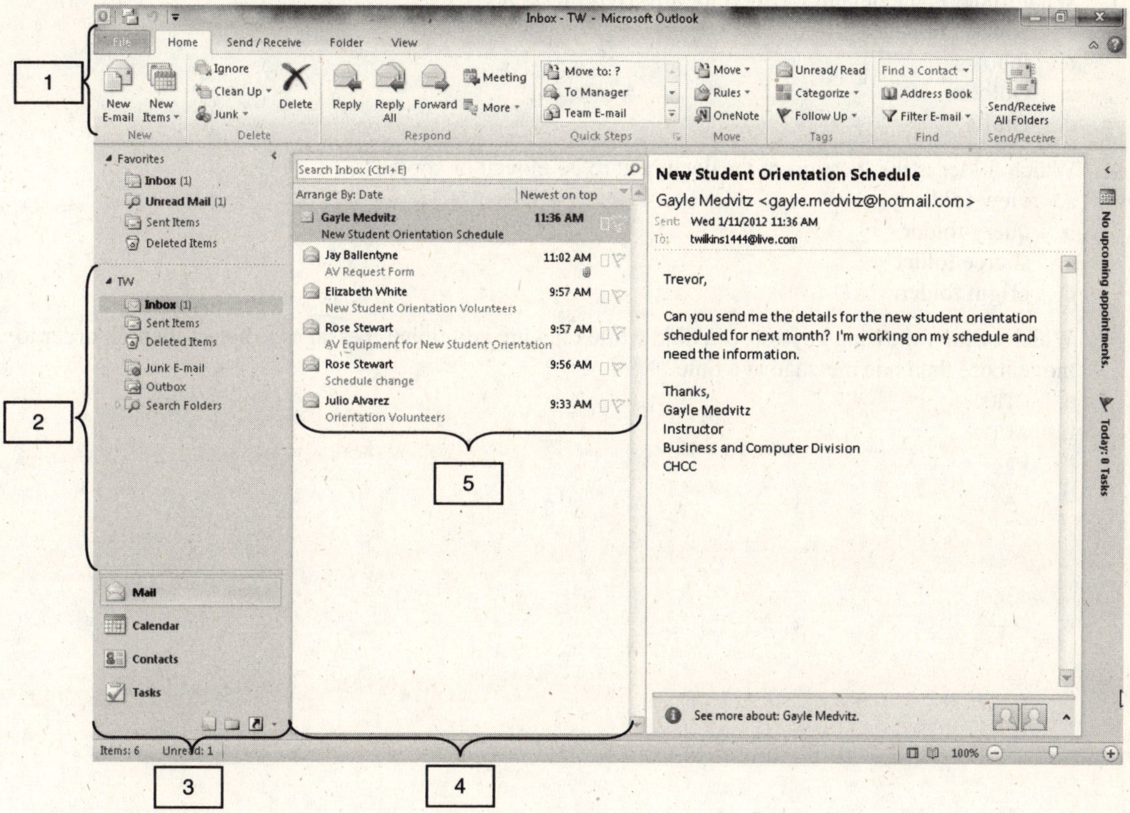

Figure OUT1

1. ____________________
2. ____________________
3. ____________________
4. ____________________
5. ____________________

Multiple Choice (5)

Circle the letter of the best answer.

1. Which of the following is the unique name associated with a specific Internet address?
   a. domain name
   b. user name
   c. password
   d. all of the above
2. Which of the following is a communications protocol?
   a. Rich Text Format
   b. HTML format
   c. Plain Text format
   d. SMTP
3. What folder is the default location for all saved messages?
   a. Saved Messages
   b. Inbox
   c. Outbox
   d. Drafts
4. Which folder is the location of the document to be moved or copied?
   a. view folder
   b. query folder
   c. source folder
   d. origin folder
5. Which of the following keys do you hold while clicking additional messages to select them in order to move more than one message at a time?
   a. CTRL
   b. ALT
   c. F5
   d. F7

Dialog Box (5)

Answer the following questions about the Add New Account dialog box in Figure OUT2.

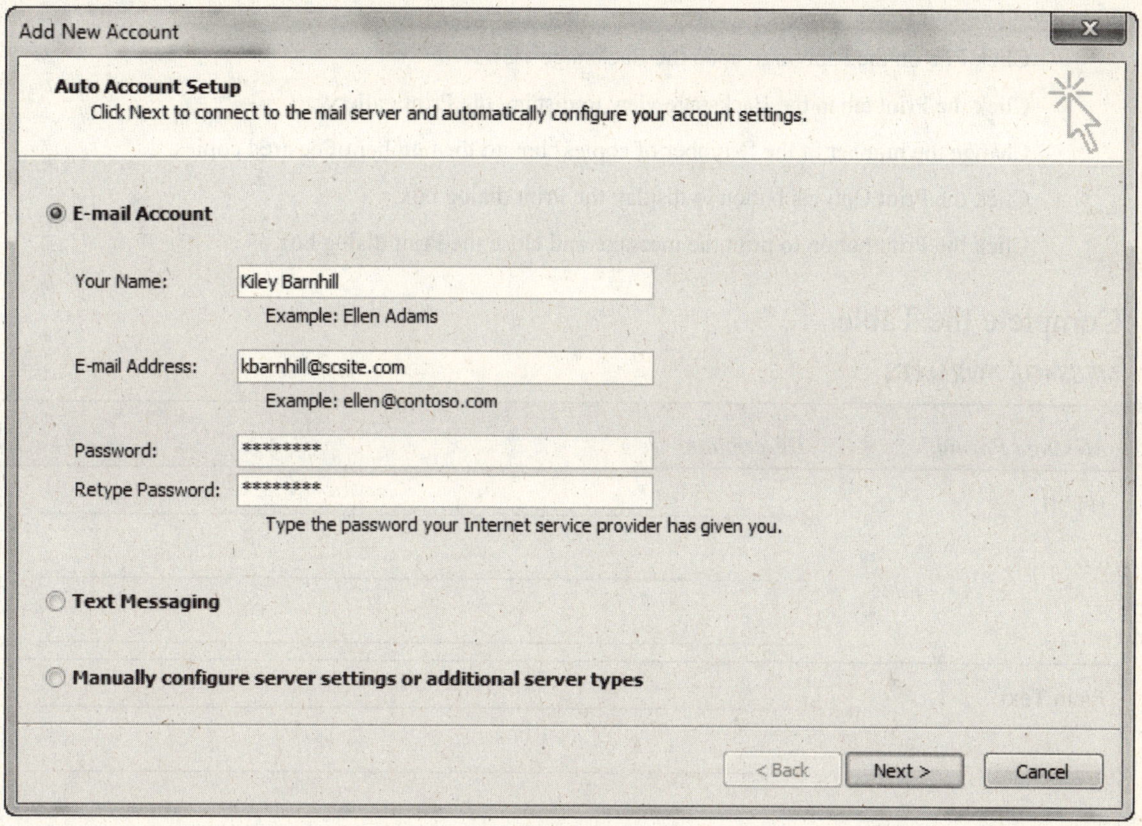

Figure OUT2

1. How was the dialog box displayed? ______________________________
2. Why is the password displayed the way that it is in the dialog box? ______________________________
3. What is the user name shown? ______________________________
4. What is the domain name shown? ______________________________
5. Why is the password retyped? ______________________________

Fill in the Blanks (5)

Write a word (or words) in the blank to complete each sentence correctly.

1. A(n) ______________________ file is a data file that stores a user's Outlook items, including e-mail messages, on the computer.
2. A(n) ______________________ is a unique combination of characters that identifies a specific e-mail user.
3. A(n) ______________ is a word, phrase, symbol, or picture in an e-mail message or on a Web page that, when clicked, directs you to another document or Web site.
4. As you type an e-mail address, the ______________________ feature begins to suggest possible matches based on names you have typed before.
5. ______________________ are containers that store Outlook items of a specific type.

Sequence (5)

Use the numbers 1 – 5 to show the order in which these steps should be performed to print multiple copies of an e-mail message.

___ Click File on the Ribbon to open the Backstage view.

___ Click the Print tab in the Backstage view to display the Print gallery.

___ Change the number in the 'Number of copies' box to the number of desired copies.

___ Click the Print Options button to display the Print dialog box.

___ Click the Print button to print the message and close the Print dialog box.

Complete the Table

MESSAGE FORMATS

Message Format	***Description***
HTML	______________________
Plain Text	______________________
Rich Text	______________________

Short Answer (5)

Write a brief answer to each question.

1. What is a virus?

2. What does the Reading Pane display?

3. To what does formatting refer?

4. Is an e-mail message permanently deleted when you click the Delete button?

5. What happens if Outlook does not have a built-in previewer for an attachment's file type?

Activities

Expanding on Apply Your Knowledge

Perform the following tasks.

1. Create a new e-mail message addressed to your instructor and enter SuperKids Nursery School Bulletin as the subject.
2. Enter Greetings! as the greeting line, checking spelling as you type.
3. Insert a blank line, and then enter It gives me great pleasure to welcome you to a new school year at SuperKids Nursery School. Classes will begin on Wednesday, September 1. Parents are encouraged to accompany their child to class on that day, so that they can meet their child's teacher and ease any anxiety that their child may be experiencing. After leaving your child, please join us in the school gymnasium, where light refreshments will be served. I look forward to seeing you on that day, and working with you to ensure that your child has an enjoyable and growth-filled year. as the message text, checking spelling as you type.
4. Insert a blank line, and then enter a two-line signature, with your name on the first line and Principal, SuperKids Nursery School as the second line.
5. Attach a document of your choosing to the e-mail message.
6. Save the e-mail message using the file name, Super Kids Nursery School Bulletin.

Expanding on the Lab

Perform the following tasks.

1. Create a new e-mail message. Address the message to yourself.
2. Enter a subject, greeting, message text, and signature of your own choosing. The message text should consist of at least two sentences. Insert a blank line between the greeting and the message text, and between the message text and the signature. If Outlook flags any misspelled words as you type, check their spelling and correct them.
3. Send the e-mail message with high importance and use the Plain Text format for the message.
4. When you receive the e-mail message, move it to a new folder in your Inbox named Urgent Messages.
5. Save the e-mail message using the file name, Urgent Message.

Microsoft Outlook 2010

Chapter Two
Managing Calendars

Overview

This chapter illustrates using Outlook to create a personal schedule by entering appointments, create recurring appointments, move appointments to new dates, and schedule events. You also learn how to invite attendees to a meeting, accept a meeting request, and propose and change the time of a meeting. To review your schedule, you learn to view and print your calendar in different views and print styles. Finally, you learn how to export your personal folder to an external storage device.

Chapter Outline

I. Introduction [OUT 50]

II. Project — Appointments, Events, and Meetings in Calendar [OUT 50]

The Calendar is ____

A. Overview [OUT 50]

As you create an appointment, event, or meeting to develop a schedule, you should follow these general guidelines:

1. ____
2. ____
3. ____
4. ____
5. ____
6. ____
7. ____

B. Calendar window [OUT 53]

The Date Navigator shows ____

The My Calendars pane includes ____

____

C. Calendar items [OUT 53]

An item is ____

Outlook defines an appointment as ____

____

Outlook defines an event as ______________________________

An appointment becomes a meeting when ______________________________

____

☞ To create a personal folder

1. ______________________________
2. ______________________________

____

____

____

3. ______________________________

☞ To display a personal calendar

1. ______________________________

____

☞ To remove the default calendar from the appointment area

1. ______________________________

____

III. Viewing the Calendar [OUT 57]

☞ To go to a specific date

1. ______________________________
2. ______________________________

____

____

3. ______________________________

☞ To display the Calendar in Work Week view

Work Week view shows ______________________________

1. ______________________________

____

☞ To display the Calendar in Week view

Week view shows ______________________________

1. ______________________________

____

☞ To display the Calendar in Month view

Month view shows ______________________________

1. ______________________________

____

____

☞ To display the Calendar in Schedule view

Schedule view shows ____________________

1. ____________________

____

2. ____________________

IV. Creating and editing appointments [OUT 61]

A. Creating appointments in the appointment area [OUT 61]

☞ To display one calendar in Day view

1. ____________________

____

☞ To create a one-time appointment using the appointment area

1. ____________________

____

____

2. ____________________

3. ____________________

B. Creating appointments using the Appointment window [OUT 64]

A recurrence pattern is ____________________

A reminder is ____________________

The appointment status is ____________________

☞ To create a one-time appointment using the Appointment window

1. ____________________

____

____

____

2. ____________________

3. ____________________

4. ____________________

____

5. ____________________

____

6. ____________________

C. Setting appointment options [OUT 66]

☞ To change the status of an appointment

1. ____________________

____

2. ______________________________

☞ To set a reminder for the appointment

1. ______________________________

2. ______________________________

☞ To save the appointment

1. ______________________________

____

D. Creating recurring appointments [OUT 71]

A recurring appointment happens at ______________________________

☞ To set recurrence options for an appointment

1. ______________________________

2. ______________________________

____

____

3. ______________________________

____

4. ______________________________

E. Using natural language phrasing [OUT 76]

A natural language phrase is ______________________________

☞ To enter an appointment date and time using natural language phrases

1. ______________________________

____

____

2. ______________________________

____

____

3. ______________________________

____

4. ______________________________

____

____

F. Editing appointments [OUT 79]

☞ To move an appointment to a different time on the same day

1. ______________________________

____

☞ To move an appointment to a different month

1.
2.
3.

☞ To delete a single occurrence of a recurring appointment

1.
2.
3.
4.

V. Creating and editing events [OUT 84]

☞ To create a one-time event in the Appointment window

1.
2.
3.
4.
5.

☞ To move a one-time event to a new date and change the event status

1. ______________________________

2. ______________________________

____

____

3. ______________________________

____

☞ To delete a one-time event

1. ______________________________

____

☞ To create a recurring event using the Appointment window

1. ______________________________

____

____

____

____

2. ______________________________

____

3. ______________________________

4. ______________________________

____

____

____

____

5. ______________________________

____

____

6. ______________________________

____

____

☞ To move a recurring event to a different day

1. ______________________________

____

2. ______________________________

____

____

____

3. ______________________________

____

☞ To delete a recurring event

1. ______________________________

2. ______________________________

3. ______________________________

4. ______________________________

VI. Creating and editing meetings [OUT 92]

The meeting organizer is ______________________________

A meeting request is ______________________________

Attendees are ______________________________

☞ To view the School Calendar in overlay mode

1. ______________________________

____

2. ______________________________

☞ To create and send a meeting request

1. ______________________________

____

2. ______________________________

____

____

____

____

3. ______________________________

____

____

4. ______________________________

____

____

☞ To change the time of a meeting and send an update

1. ______________________________

____

____

2. ______________________________

☞ To reply to a meeting request

1. ______________________________

2. ______________________________

3. ______________________________

☞ To propose a new meeting time

1. ______________________________
2. ______________________________
3. ______________________________
4. ______________________________
5. ______________________________
6. ______________________________

☞ To change the time of a one-time meeting and send an update

1. ______________________________
2. ______________________________
3. ______________________________

☞ To cancel a meeting

1. ______________________________
2. ______________________________
3. ______________________________

VII. Printing calendars in different views [OUT 99]

Print styles are ______________________________

A hard copy (or printout) is ______________________________

☞ To print the calendar in Weekly Calendar style

1. ______________________________

2. ______

☞ To change the current view to List view

1. ______

2. ______

☞ To print the calendar from List view

1. ______
2. ______
3. ______
4. ______
5. ______
6. ______

VIII. Exporting and importing folders [OUT 104]

Outlook uses the Import and Export Wizard to ______

Exporting is ______

Importing is ______

A .pst file is ______

☞ To export a subfolder to a USB flash drive

1. ______

2. ______
3. ______

4. ______

5. ______

6. ____

____

7. ____

____

8. ____

☞ To import a personal subfolder

1. ____
2. ____
3. ____
4. ____
5. ____
6. ____
7. ____
8. ____
9. ____
10. ____
11. ____

☞ To delete a personal subfolder

1. ____

____

2. ____

Review

Matching (5)

Match each term on the left with the best description from the right.

___ 1. recurring meeting

___ 2. recurring appointment

___ 3. recurring event

___ 4. one-time meeting

___ 5. one-time event

a. a staff meeting would be an example

b. includes people and other resources, like meeting rooms

c. a holiday would be an example

d. occurs at least once and lasts 24 hours or longer, such as a vacation or a conference

e. occurs at regular intervals, such as weekly, biweekly, monthly, or bimonthly

f. a default calendar item

g. involves only your schedule and does not invite other attendees or require resources such as a conference room

True-False (5)

*Circle **T** if the statement is true and **F** if the statement is false.*

T F 1. You cannot use Outlook to print a daily, weekly, or monthly calendar; you must use Microsoft Word for that.

T F 2. The appointment area displays 10-minute time slots by default when viewing Calendar in Day, Work Week, or Week view and is not available in Month view.

T F 3. Outlook can convert abbreviations and ordinal numbers into complete words and dates.

T F 4. If you move a recurring appointment, all instances of the appointment move as well.

T F 5. When a meeting request arrives in an attendee's Inbox, it displays the same icon as a regular e-mail message.

Modified True-False (5)

*Circle **T** if the statement is true. If the statement is <u>false</u>, circle **F** and make the statement true by writing the replacement for the underlined word or phrase in the blank.*

T F 1. Outlook defines a(n) <u>meeting</u> as an activity that occurs at least once and lasts 24 hours or longer.

____

T F 2. By default, Outlook shows a one-time event as <u>busy</u>.

____

T F 3. <u>Busy</u> time is marked with a slashed bar in Day, Week, Work Week, or Month view.

____

T F 4. All or part of a calendar can be printed in a number of different print <u>styles</u>.

____

T F 5. Adding a subfolder to your Outlook mailbox is called <u>exporting</u>.

____

Definitions (5)

Briefly define each term.

1. Calendar ______________________________
2. appointment ______________________________
3. Month view ______________________________
4. reminder ______________________________
5. attendees ______________________________

The Outlook Window (5)

Identify the elements indicated in Figure OUT3.

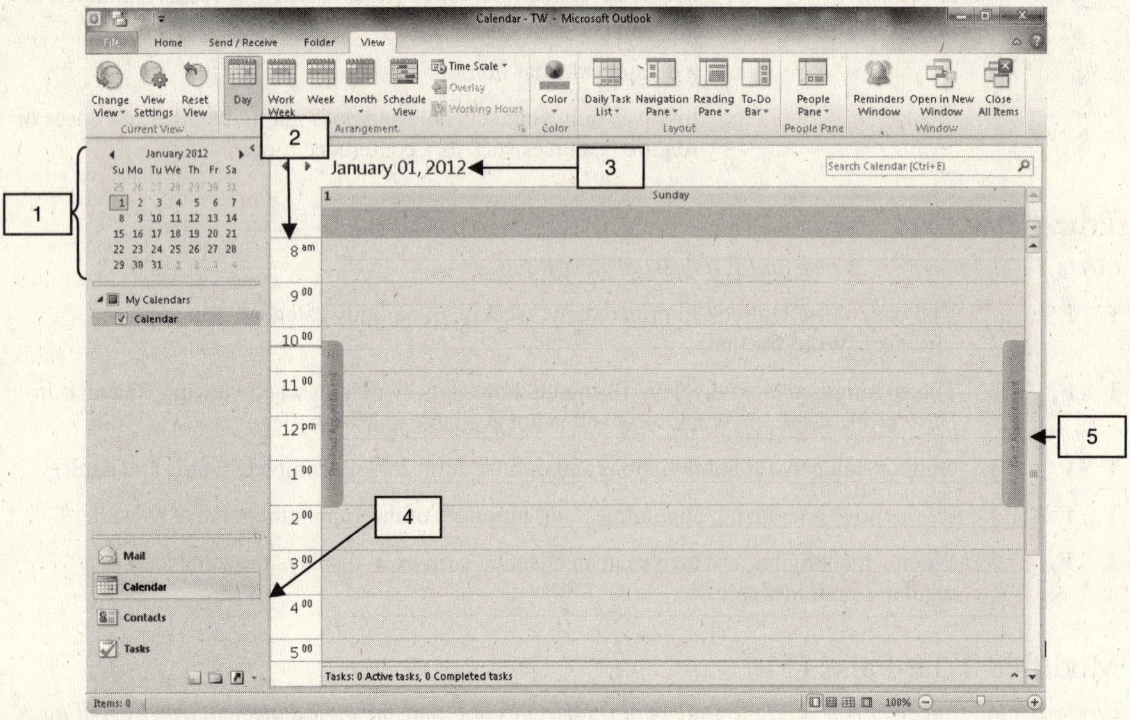

Figure OUT3

1. ______________________ 4. ______________________
2. ______________________ 5. ______________________
3. ______________________

Multiple Choice (5)

Circle the letter of the best answer.

1. Which pane includes a list of available calendars where you can view a single calendar or view additional calendars side by side?
   a. All Calendars pane
   b. My Calendars pane
   c. Global Calendars pane
   d. Quick Calendar view
2. Which of the following is any element in Outlook that contains information?
   a. icon
   b. unit
   c. target
   d. item
3. What is the term for the layout in which each Microsoft Outlook 2010 folder displays the items it contains?
   a. view
   b. scene
   c. pane
   d. landscape
4. What is the term for how the time for a calendar item is marked on your calendar?
   a. appointment view
   b. appointment target
   c. appointment source
   d. appointment status
5. What is the term for the person who creates the meeting and sends the invitation?
   a. founder
   b. organizer
   c. source
   d. initiator

Calendar (5)

Answer the following questions about the Calendar window in Figure OUT4.

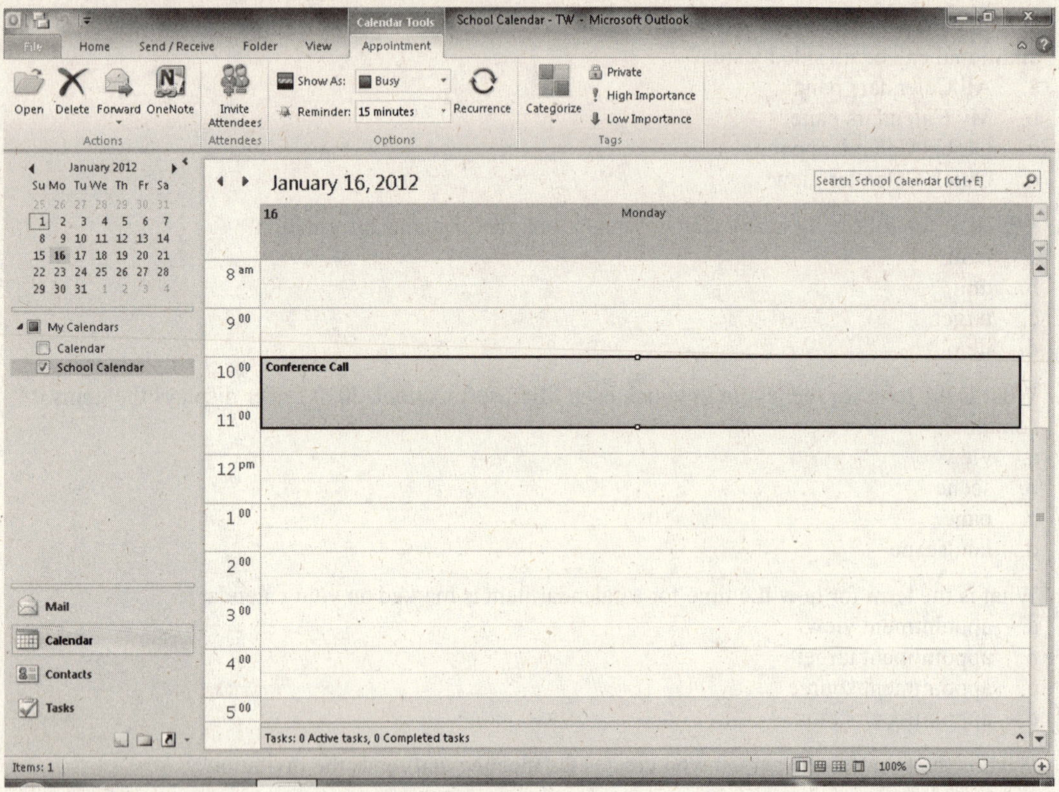

Figure OUT4

1. What are the white dots on the selected appointment? ______________________________
2. Do you have to save the appointment entry shown? ______________________________
3. Why is Busy showing in the Show As box? ______________________________
4. Why does the date of the conference call appointment appear in bold on the Date Navigator? ________ ______________________________
5. After typing Conference Call as the appointment subject, what key do you press to add the appointment in the appointment area? ______________________________

Fill in the Blanks (5)

Write a word (or words) in the blank to complete each sentence correctly.

1. A(n) ______________________ is a list of items to be discussed in a meeting.
2. A(n) ______________________ becomes a meeting when people and other resources are invited.
3. The ______________ pattern schedules the Outlook appointment on the calendar at regular intervals for a designated period of time.
4. A meeting ______________________ is an e-mail invitation to the meeting and arrives in each attendee's Inbox.
5. Transferring a subfolder to a USB flash drive is called ______________________.

Sequence (5)

Use the numbers 1 – 5 to show the order in which these steps should be performed to propose a new meeting time.

___ Click the Send button.

___ Click the Propose time button.

___ Click the appropriate meeting request to display the Calendar Tools Meeting Occurrence tab on the Ribbon.

___ Click the Propose New Time button and then click the Tentative and Propose New Time option.

___ Drag through the time slot that you want to propose.

Complete the Table

CALENDAR ITEM STATUS OPTIONS

Calendar Item Status Option	***Description***
Free	______________________________ ______________________________
Tentative	______________________________ ______________________________
Busy	______________________________ ______________________________
Out of Office	______________________________ ______________________________

Short Answer (5)

Write a brief answer to each question.

1. What does Work Week view show?

2. What does Schedule View display?

3. What is a natural language phrase?

4. In what way do events differ from appointments?

5. What is the function of the Import and Export Wizard?

Activities

Expanding on Apply Your Knowledge

Perform the following tasks.

1. In the Outlook Calendar window, display the Apply Your Knowledge 2-1 Calendar that you created in Apply Your Knowledge. Use Work Week view to display the calendar.
2. Reschedule the work on February 16 to February 17. The work starts at 11:00 AM and continues until 3:00 PM.
3. Add a one-hour History Discussion Section on Monday mornings from 10:00 AM – 11:00 AM in HST 133.
4. Change the location of the Chemistry Study Lab from CHM 225 to CHM 117.
5. Print the final calendar in Month view.

Expanding on the Lab

Perform the following tasks.

1. In the Outlook Calendar window, display the English Department Birthdays Calendar that you created in In the Lab 1. Use the Calendar Details style to display the calendar.
2. Correct Brett Lipinski's birthday. Instead of 2/17, it should be 2/15.
3. Add the birthdays of two new employees:
   - Perry Petrilli, who was born on 10/21/1985
   - Melia Rylan, who was born on 6/19/1978

   For each event, show the time as Free, set the reminder to one day, and set the event to recur yearly on the same day. Each event should be an all-day event.
4. Because Madelyn Judowski's birthday is during a month when many people are away on vacation, change the reminder for her birthday to one month.
5. Print the revised calendar using the Calendar Details style.